Wil

The Myth of the Noble Eco-Savage

Robert Whelan

Published by the IEA Environment Unit, 1999

First published in May 1999 by
The Environment Unit
The Institute of Economic Affairs
2 Lord North Street
Westminster
London SW1P 3LB

IEA Studies on the Environment No. 14
All rights reserved
ISBN 0-255 36447-4

Many IEA publications are translated into languages other
than English or are reprinted. Permission to translate or to
reprint should be sought from the General Director at the
address above.

Printed in Great Britain by
St Edmundsbury Press
Bury St Edmunds, Suffolk

Set in Times New Roman and Univers

**In memory of
Julian Simon
who dispelled so many myths**

Contents

Foreword   *Will Sweetman*   vi

The Author   viii

Acknowledgements   viii

1.   **A Short View of Savagery**   1

      Admirable Cannibals   2

      The Progress of Savagery   6

      As Free as Nature First Made Man   10

      From Fiction to Faction   11

      Citizen Savage   15

      In Search of a New Role   19

2.   **The Noble Eco-Savage**   20

      Salad Days   20

      From Hero to Villain   23

      Paradise Lost   25

3.   **History vs. Mythology**   28

      The Age of Innocence?   28

      The Population Implosion   29

      Making a Bonfire of the Forests   30

      When Conservation Does Not Make Sense   33

      Extinction is Forever   34

      The Overkill Hypothesis   35

      Sustainable Harvest?   37

	Environmentalist Him Speak with Forked Tongue	41
	Dances in Wolfshit	42
4.	**Treading Lightly on the Earth**	**47**
	Kayapo Inc.	49
	Disappointed Expectations	50
	Empirical Evidence and the Piro	51
	Only Slaves Climb Trees	53
	A Serious Case of Entrapment	55
5.	**From Arcadia to Utopia**	**59**
	'One or Two People Want to Go There'	59
	Gold Fever	60
	The Gentle Tasaday	62
	The Land of Lost Content	66
	Index	**68**

Foreword

The history of European exploration and expansion in the last five centuries reveals shifts in European attitudes towards the peoples with whom Europe came into contact. The early glowing accounts of them as gentle innocents gave way by the late eighteenth century to an attempt to rank the peoples of the world according to how closely they approximated to a European ideal of civilisation. The Scots, conscious of their own nation's recent reputation for barbarity, were particularly keen to show 'how, from being a savage, man rose to be a Scotchman'.[1] The attempt was nevertheless underpinned by a belief in the uniformity of human nature. William Robertson, historian and leader of the Moderate faction in the Church of Scotland, expressed the belief thus:

> 'A human being as he comes originally from the hand of nature, is everywhere the same. At his first appearance in the state of infancy, whether it be among the rudest savages, or in the most civilized nations, we can discern no quality which marks any distinction or superiority. The capacity of improvement seems to be the same and the talents he may afterwards acquire, as well as the virtues he may be rendered capable of exercising, depend, in a great measure, upon the state of society in which he is placed...' [2]

In the nineteenth century, a more chauvinist mood prevailed; in our own century we have, as Robert Whelan ably shows, come full circle and returned to a utopian view of non-European, particularly American and Australasian, peoples. What is most noticeable in this history of attitudes to other peoples, which is only beginning to be written, is that it depends far more on changes in European society and self-perception than on any changes in the nature of its supposed objects.

It is against this background that we should understand that

---

[1] Walter Bagehot, *Estimates of some Englishmen and Scotsmen* (1858). Bagehot had in mind particularly *The Wealth of Nations*.

[2] *History of America* (2 vols. London, 1777) I: 401-2.

most pervasive of modern myths: the myth of the noble savage. The use of the innocent or the outsider as a literary device to critique a present state of affairs has had a long history, and not only in Western literature.[3] Like all really good myths, the myth of the noble savage can been turned to serve many different interests, from those of Colombus to those of the eighteenth-century *philosophes*, in whose hands it became just another stick with which to beat the church. In our own time it has served numerous ends, including the sexual revolution and most recently the Green agenda. While the Greens' use of the noble savage as the ideal conservationist is as indiscriminate as any other, what makes their use of the myth particularly pernicious is that, unlike the supposed authors of Voltaire's *Lettre d'un Turc* or Montesquieu's *Lettres Persanes*, who were understood to be fictions, the noble savage in his most recent Green incarnation is supposed really to exist (or, when he cannot be found, at least *to have existed* prior to his corruption by Western civilisation).

It is therefore necessary patiently to undermine the foundations of this myth, both by revealing its specific history in modern European discourse and by trying to take a view of indigenous peoples which is not contaminated by the presupposition that they are by nature either more or less noble than us. Both these requirements are superbly executed in Robert Whelan's timely and highly readable account of the noble savage myth. He also demonstrates the great importance of debunking this particular myth by analysing some of the disastrous consequences of the inevitable failure of contemporary 'noble savages' to live up to it.

April 1999   *WILL SWEETMAN*
                                               Middlesex University

March 1999   *ROGER BATE*
                                               Director, IEA Environment Unit

---

[3] The same technique is used in Mahayana Buddhist texts to critique the learning of Theravadin monks.

The Author

Robert Whelan is the Assistant Director of the IEA Health and Welfare Unit. His books include *Mounting Greenery*, IEA 1988; *Choices in Childbearing*, Committee on Population and the Economy 1992; *Broken Homes and Battered Children* and *Teaching Sex in Schools*, Family Education Trust 1994 and 1995; *The Cross and the Rainforest* (with Joseph Kirwan and Paul Haffner), Acton Institute and Eerdmans 1996; and, for the IEA Health and Welfare Unit, *Making a Lottery of Good Causes* (with Roger Cummins) 1995, *The Corrosion of Charity* 1996, *Octavia Hill and the Social Housing Debate* (ed.) 1998 and *Involuntary Action* 1999.

Acknowledgements

I must first of all acknowledge my indebtedness to Dr Alejandro Chafuen, President of the Atlas Economic Research Foundation in Fairfax, Virginia, his directors and staff, especially Dr Jo Kwong. Without the financial support and personal kindness which they extended to me as an Atlas Summer Research Fellow this book could not have been written. I am indebted to Sean Gabb for research assistance, and to Elaine Hawley, Librarian of the Institute for Humane Studies at George Mason University in Fairfax, Virginia, for locating material. Robert Royal of the Institute for Ethics and Public Policy gave helpful advice about Christopher Columbus. Thanks are also due to Ron Brunton, David Murray, Charles Kay, Patricia Morgan, Matt Ridley and Julian Morris for supplying me with helpful material. I bear sole responsibility for the conclusions. Needless to say, like all IEA authors, I have benefited from the comments of those who participate in the anonymous refereeing process.

I am as free as nature first made man,
Ere the base laws of servitude began,
When wild in woods the noble savage ran.

John Dryden, The Conquest of Granada

1. A Short View of Savagery

'These things never happen and are always true.'[1]

SALLUST

On 3 August 1492 Christopher Columbus set sail from Spain for 'the Indies' – that is to say, the Far East, including China and Japan – with letters of greeting from the King and Queen of Spain to the Great Khan of Cathay. However, instead of heading east as usual, he went west, on the assumption that the world was round. Columbus was not the first person to make this assumption, but he was probably the first to risk a sea journey across what was believed to be an immense stretch of water between Europe's western coast and Asia's eastern one. No one realised that America lay between the two, and when Columbus reached land he assumed that he had been successful in finding the western route to the Indies, never apparently realising that he had actually arrived at another continent. The naming of the West Indies, and the description of the native Americans as Indians, reflected this initial mistake.

However, it seems that Columbus may have made another mistake which had more serious consequences. He was so overwhelmed by the majesty of the landscape that he thought he had found the site of the Garden of Eden. He mistook the mouth of the Orinoco river in modern-day Venezuela for the entrance to the Earthly Paradise, in accordance with a theological tradition that God had not destroyed the Garden of Eden but preserved it, somewhere on earth, as a haven free from suffering and death.[2]

---

[1] Sallust, *Of Gods and of the Earth*, Chapter 2: *Quae enim semper sunt, nunquam fiunt: semper vero sunt.*

[2] A. Rosenblat, *La primera visión de América y otros estudios*, Caracas: Ministerio de Educacion, 1965, quoted in C. Rangel, *The Latin Americans: Their Love-Hate*

Columbus himself described the natives of the Caribbean to King Ferdinand and Queen Isabella of Spain in such glowing terms that they sounded as if they were living in a state of pre-lapsarian innocence:

> 'I assure Your Highnesses that I believe that in all the world there is no better people nor better country. They love their neighbours as themselves, and they have the sweetest talk in the world, and are gentle and always laughing... these people have no religion whatever, nor are they idolaters, but rather they are very meek and know no evil. They do not kill or capture others and are without weapons.'[3]

Of course, Columbus was obliged to put the most optimistic gloss on his discoveries for the benefit of his royal paymasters, and if he had any illusions about the simple and uncorrupted goodness of the American Indians he was soon disabused. However, stories about the inhabitants of the New World began to circulate in Europe, where they took on the tone of an Arcadian idyll.

These simple primitives enjoyed a warm reception throughout the European world of letters, but it was in France that they found their most enthusiastic following. The poet Ronsard depicted America as 'a "Western Arcadia", free from the numbing artificiality of French court life. At Rouen, a troupe of Brazilian Indians performed a masque before Charles IX....Among those who met and conversed with them after the show was the philosopher Michel de Montaigne.'[4]

Admirable Cannibals

It was Montaigne who was to give to the idea of people living in a state of innocence its first fully-fledged exposition. In his essay *On the Cannibals*, published in 1580, he provided the blueprint

---

Relationship with the United States, New Brunswick, N.J.: Transaction Books, 1987, p.10.

[3] Quoted in R. Royal, *Columbus on Trial: 1492 v. 1992*, Herndon, VA: Young Americas Foundation, 1992, p.2.

[4] C. Nicholl, *The Creature in the Map: A Journey to El Dorado*, London: Jonathan Cape, 1995, p.299.

for a whole literature, philosophy, anthropology and sociology which we can sum up in the phrase: The Noble Savage.

Montaigne claimed to have based his observations mainly on an account of the Brazilian Indians which he had received from a man who had spent 10 or 12 years with them.[5] He also mentioned meeting an Indian after the performance in Rouen, but said that his translator had been so unsatisfactory that he had learnt little. His account, therefore, laid no claim to first-hand experience, but Montaigne emphasised the simple honesty of his anonymous informant who had, as far as he could see, no axe to grind. It is possible that this was a literary distancing device to protect himself from being blamed for any errors in the account, but, however he came by the information, Montaigne appears to have been the victim of a massive leg-pull.

> '[T]hose people have no trade of any kind, no acquaintance with writing, no knowledge of numbers, no terms for governor or political superior, no practice of subordination or of riches or poverty, no contracts, no inheritances, no divided estates, no occupation but leisure...no clothing, no agriculture, no metals, no use of wine or corn. Among them you hear no words for treachery, lying, cheating, avarice, envy, backbiting or forgiveness.'[6]

Montaigne's account of their ways of passing the time is equally idyllic:

> 'They spend the whole day dancing; the younger men go off hunting with bow and arrow. Meanwhile some of the women-folk are occupied in warming up their drink: that is their main task.'[7]

Montaigne does not claim that they are pacifist, but that they only go to war to demonstrate their courage. They have no need to conquer new lands:

> '...since without toil or travail they still enjoy that bounteous Nature who furnishes them abundantly with all they need...They are still in

---

[5] Durand de Villegagnon had landed in Brazil in 1557.

[6] See M. Montaigne, 'On the Cannibals', from *The Essays of Michel de Montaigne*, trans. M. A. Screech, Allen Lane, The Penguin Press, 1991, p.233.

[7] *Ibid.*, p.234.

that blessed state of desiring nothing beyond what is ordained by their natural necessities: for them anything further is merely superfluous.'[8]

Montaigne notes their practice of cannibalism, from which the essay takes it title, and which he describes as 'horrible barbarity',[9] but he quickly contrasts it with the 'treachery, disloyalty, tyranny and cruelty, which are everyday vices in us'. It was this unfavourable comparison of civilisation with savagery which gave Montaigne's short essay the claim to being first in the field. Other writers and travellers had described the idyllic lifestyles of the American Indians: Montaigne gave the legend the twist which was to make it distinctive. He turned the fantastic world of the savages into the gold standard against which Western civilisation would be judged and found wanting. 'It is no lie to say that these men are indeed savages – by our standards; for either they must be or we must be: there is an amazing gulf between their souls and ours.' The concept of savagery thus becomes entirely relative.

In order to describe his uncorrupted Indians, Montaigne inserts a verse from Virgil:

'Hos natura modos primum dedit.'
'These are the ways which nature first ordained.'[10]

thus neatly linking his account of the Brazilian Indians to the long tradition of the Golden Age which was supposed by authors and philosophers to have preceded the present degenerate state of the world. This was the age when, as Ovid put it:

'The earth itself, without compulsion, untouched by hoe or ploughshare, of herself gave all things needful.'[11]

---

[8] *Ibid.*, p.236.

[9] *Ibid.*, p.235.

[10] Virgil, *The Georgics*, II, 20. English quotations are taken from the translation by K. R. Mackenzie, published by the Folio Society, London, in 1969. Montaigne took the verse seriously out of context. Virgil was describing the ways in which trees propagate themselves in the wild.

Belief in a Golden Age is common to both the classical and the Judeo-Christian traditions, but for both it is in the past.[12] For Jews and Christians, Adam and Eve were expelled from the Garden of Eden a long time ago, and the way back was barred by an angel bearing a fiery sword.[13] Nor did Ovid's readers in ancient Rome take his descriptions of a fertile landscape pushing up its fruits unbidden as a representation of the world as it was in their own time. These were memories of an age long past.[14] When Virgil wrote of sheep with fleeces which would change colour spontaneously to save us the bother of dyeing our woollies,[15] this was intended as a prophecy of a new Golden Age to come. For both biblical and pagan authors, the real-life world was one in which you had to work hard to get anything from nature.[16]

It was necessary, therefore, to make an intellectual gear-change to modify the Golden Age tradition to accommodate the noble savage, which Montaigne did not invent but which he could be said to have codified. The Golden Age recalled a long-lost country of the imagination, but Montaigne claimed to be describing the actual living conditions of Indians in contemporary Brazil. It was the here-and-now, not the once-

---

[11] Ovid, *Metamorphoses*, I, 100.

[12] It is necessary to distinguish between the literature of the Golden Age and the more fanciful tradition of pastoral poetry, which emphasises all the nice things about the countryside, like mossy banks and purling streams, and leaves out the mosquitoes and the nettles. Although pastoral poetry can be charming, no one really imagines that country life is like that, any more than devotees of grand opera imagine that in real life people sing their way through crises. In any case, pastoral poets, from Ovid to Alexander Pope, have been notorious townies.

[13] 'There is no eternal city for us in this life, but we look for one in the life to come.' (Heb. 13.14).

[14] In Plato's dialogue the eponymous Critias describes a golden age in Greece when the land belonged to brother-and-sister deities Athene and Hephaistos, who taught their 'children of the soil' the best modes of husbandry in an ideal landscape.

[15] Eclogue IV, 42-3.

[16] 'Cursed is the ground because of you; through painful toil you will eat of it all the days of your life.' (Gen. 3:17).
'The father of mankind himself has willed
The path of husbandry should not be smooth.' (Georgics I: 125).

upon-a-time. In fact, Montaigne might as well have included the fauns and centaurs of Arcadia in his landscape for all the resemblance which his account bore to real life. However, it was because the accounts of the native peoples of Columbus's New World were so successfully grafted onto a venerable Western literary tradition that the legend became so potent. According to Carlos Rangel, who discussed the impact of the noble savage myth in his book *The Latin Americans*:

> '...the discovery of America brought nothing to European mythology that was not already there; it only rekindled old dreams of a Golden Age and the State of Innocence that preceded the Fall...The newcomers, in their search, created the most powerful myth of modern times: that of the noble savage. This is the "Americanized" version of the myth of man's innocence before the Fall, and that new version of the myth was to have an immense impact on the history of ideas.'[17]

Rangel makes the point that the American Indians were not the first 'native peoples' with whom Europeans came into contact. The northern parts of Africa had been accessible to European cultures since the days of the Roman Empire, and black faces were not unfamiliar in European cities by the fifteenth century, but Africans were not regarded as noble savages:

> 'Why did Europeans not encounter the noble savage in Africa? Quite certainly because the African savages had been known since antiquity and were not, therefore, truly exotic. *Europe found no noble savages in Africa because it was not seeking them there.* And this is why the blacks were perceived by Western consciousness simply as savages – without qualification, in the exact, pejorative meaning of the word.'[18]

The Progress of Savagery

The myth of the noble savage has proved to be a recurrent theme in Western intellectual life ever since. It has animated one of the central debates of Western culture: the question of whether

---

[17] C. Rangel, *op.cit.*, pp.12-13.

[18] *Ibid.*, p. 13n. (emphasis added)

civilisation is a good thing or a bad thing. Are men naturally good, and corrupted by the artificial nature of society, or are they naturally depraved and in need of the civilising influence of laws and religion? Do we incline towards virtue or vice?

These are questions of the most profound significance, as they affect the way in which we regard ourselves and our societies. The news which began to percolate back to Europe after the arrival of Columbus and other explorers in the New World gave the debate new vigour, because it seemed to offer the possibility of demonstration and proof. If people in the New World really were living in a state of primitive innocence, in which laws, religion and social status were unknown and irrelevant, then it was game set and match to the naturists.

Interest in the noble savage has not been constant: it comes and goes according to both contemporary events and intellectual fashions. In 1610 some strange travellers' tales ignited the debate in England and led to the first major literary work in English to deal with the subject of savage life: Shakespeare's *The Tempest*.

In the previous year a fleet of ships carrying 500 colonists set out from England to join John Smith's Virginia Colony in the New World. One of the ships, carrying the Admiral and the newly-appointed governor of Virginia, was separated from the rest in a storm and was presumed lost. However, in the following year the missing colonists arrived safely in Virginia, telling of wonderful adventures in the Bermudas, where the ship had run ashore. They gave reports of a warm and fertile landscape, inhabited by friendly natives, which were soon absorbed into the literary tradition of the Golden Age. A batch of pamphlets appeared in London where the wonderful happenings became the talk of the town, and at least some of these provided Shakespeare with source material for *The Tempest*.[19] At some stage between

---

[19] In his introduction to the Arden edition of the play (1954) Frank Kermode identifies three accounts which Shakespeare must have seen: *Discovery of the Barmudas* by Sylvester Jourdain (1610); the Council of Virginia's *True Declaration of the state of the Colonie in Virginia, with a confutation of such scandalous reports as have tended to the disgrace of so worthy an enterprise* (1610); and *True Reportory of the Wrack* by William Strachey (1625). Although the last was not published until long after the composition of *The Tempest* it seems Shakespeare may have seen it in manuscript.

the autumn of 1610, when the reports arrived in London, and November 1611, when King James had *The Tempest* performed at court, Shakespeare put the Bermuda pamphlets together with other sources to produce his final observations on the nature *vs.* nurture debate which had occupied him throughout his career.[20]

We know that Shakespeare had read Montaigne's essay *On The Cannibals* in John Florio's English translation of 1603,[21] because Gonzalo's speech, in which he describes how he would rule the island were he king, is taken almost word for word from one of Montaigne's key passages:

'   ... no kind of traffic
Would I admit; no name of magistrate;
Letters should not be known; riches, poverty,
and use of service, none...
            .... but nature should bring forth,
Of its own kind, all foison, all abundance,
To feed my innocent people.'[22]

However, it was never on the cards that Shakespeare was going to come down on the side of the noble savage. He had always been impressed by the need for order, control and authority ('Take but degree away, untune that string, And hark what discord follows'[23]) and he immediately deflates Gonzalo's beautiful speech by having Antonio point out that Gonzalo is proposing an ideal society in which there will be no distinctions of rank – except that Gonzalo will have to be king to bring it about! Gonzalo then admits that he was only fantasising to amuse his companions.

---

[20] Many scholars have seen *The Tempest*, probably rightly, as Shakespeare's conscious farewell to the stage. Prospero's snapping of his staff at the conclusion of the play, which brings his magical powers to an end, can be taken as symbolising Shakespeare's renunciation of his art. He spent his remaining years as a prosperous man of property in Stratford upon Avon.

[21] The British Museum Library has a copy of Florio's translation of Montaigne bearing the signature 'Wllm Shakspere'. Although the authenticity of the signature has been disputed it was there in 1780 when Capell first drew attention to the use which Shakespeare had made of Montaigne in *The Tempest*.

[22] *The Tempest*, II, i, 144-160 (Arden edition, 1954).

[23] *Troilus and Cressida*, I, iii, 109-110 (Arden edition, 1998).

The savage lifestyle is represented in the play by Caliban, and he is certainly not noble. He is described in the cast list as a 'salvage [savage] deformed slave'. He is lustful, slothful and untrustworthy, and, although Shakespeare allows him his moments of pathos, he is certainly not being held up for admiration. Shakespeare had clearly read Montaigne and disagreed with him. In fact it has been suggested by some critics that *The Tempest* was conceived as a satirical response to *On The Cannibals* and Montaigne's view that a society unencumbered by laws, authority and private property could be an admirable one.[24] Caliban, whose name is an obvious anagram of cannibal, looks back to the Wild Man of medieval mythology, those strange, hairy creatures who turn up on misericords in medieval churches to frighten people with the prospect of life unregulated by religion.[25]

In the most famous lines in the play Prospero's daughter Miranda, who has grown up on the island without seeing any human beings other than her father, is confronted by the King of Naples and his followers:

> 'O, wonder!
> How many goodly creatures are there here!
> How beauteous mankind is! O brave new world,
> That has such people in't!'

To which Prospero, who knows a good deal about the treachery of the royal party, makes the world-weary reply: 'Tis new to thee'.[26] His disappointment would be shared by many who subsequently based their dealings with the native peoples of new-found lands on the assumption that they were noble savages.[27]

---

[24] See, for example, A. Lovejoy, *Essays in the History of Ideas*, 1948, p.238. Lovejoy called *On The Cannibals* 'the *locus classicus* of primitivism in modern literature'.

[25] 'Salvage', the original spelling of savage, which appears in the cast list of *The Tempest*, reflects the derivation of the word from the Latin *silva* (wood). Woods and forests were frightening places to the medieval mind, beyond the civilising influence of court and city.

[26] *The Tempest*, V, i, 181-4 (Arden edition, 1954).

[27] In 1768 Louis-Antoine de Bougainville discovered Tahiti and compared it to the Garden of Eden. Captain Cook visited it the next year and brought back the usual tales

As Free as Nature First Made Man

The first usage of the expression 'noble savage' occurred in John Dryden's play *The Conquest of Granada*, performed at the Theatre Royal, Drury Lane, in 1669. The character of Almanzor, a 'moor', says of himself:

'I am as free as nature first made man,
Ere the base laws of servitude began,
When wild in woods the noble savage ran.'[28]

However, the play is a standard Restoration heroic tragedy, and does not pursue the theme of the noble savage as a critique of Western civilisation. The first fully-fledged panegyric on the noble savage in English literature was penned by Dryden's close contemporary, the notorious Mrs Aphra Behn. Her short novel *Oronooko*, published in 1678, tells the story of an African prince who is kidnapped by slavers and sold to a plantation owner in Surinam. He leads a revolt of the slaves against their masters and is tricked into surrendering by the false promise of a pardon. He is then executed, using extreme cruelty and torture.

Oronooko is classic noble savage stuff. Every twist of the plot is designed to contrast the purity and nobility of the Africans and Indians with the perfidy of the European characters. Oronooko himself, a man of such strict honour and gentlemanly behaviour as was rarely seen in England before Thomas Arnold's Rugby, is amazed that the Europeans will promise and swear to things and then break their word. He attributes this to the nature of Christianity, which is treated throughout the story as a religion of rogues and hypocrites. According to Mrs Behn, the chastity and sense of honour of the young native peoples was such that:

---

of a life free of hunger, shame or toil. Soon the real nature of Tahitian society began to emerge, with its human sacrifice, ritual infanticide and rigid class structures. The Comte de la Pérouse, who went looking for the noble savage, was bitterly disappointed and wrote: 'The most daring rascals of all Europe are less hypocritical than the natives of these islands. All their caresses were false.' (See M. Ridley, *The Origins of Virtue*, London: Viking, 1996, p.255.)

[28] Act I, Scene I.

'...the only crime and sin with a woman, is, to turn her off, to abandon her to want, shame and misery: such ill morals are only practis'd in Christian countries, where they prefer the bare name of religion; and, without vertue or morality, think that sufficient......these people represented to me an absolute idea of the first state of innocence, before man knew how to sin: And 'tis most evident and plain, that simple nature is the most harmless, inoffensive and vertuous mistress. 'Tis she alone, if she were permitted, that better instructs the world, than all the inventions of man: religion wou'd here but destroy that tranquillity they possess by ignorance; and laws wou'd but teach 'em to know offence, of which they now have no notion.'[29]

Aphra Behn is chiefly remembered now as the first woman to make her living as a writer in English, and as a result she has become a heroine of the new academic discipline of 'gender studies'. Her modern advocates promote her as a radical proto-feminist, concerned with sexual politics. However, there was nothing about her views on sexual relationships to distinguish her from her rival (male) authors of the Restoration period. Her most convincing claim to originality must lie in her development of what was to become a standard literary form: the noble savage story in which the supposed simplicity and innocence of native peoples is used as a foil to criticise aspects of sophisticated European society.

From Fiction to Faction

Oronooko was described on its title page as 'A True History', and was supposed to be based on Aphra Behn's experiences in Surinam where she claimed her father had been governor. Unfortunately Mrs Behn was such a compulsive liar that there is scarcely any fact concerning her life about which we can be sure, but of one thing we can be quite certain: the noble Africans and Indians she described were to be found only in her own imagination, and not in any geographical location.

However, she started a trend with her confusion of fact and fiction. Subsequent authors of noble savage fictions were

---

[29] Aphra Behn, *Oronooko or the Royal Slave: A True History*, first published in 1678, included in P. Henderson (ed.), *Shorter Novels of the Seventeenth Century*, London: J.M. Dent and Sons, 1967, pp.156 and 149-50.

inclined to claim a factual basis for their works, while the authors of supposedly factual works, like travel books and works of social science, found it difficult to resist the temptation to stray into the realms of fable and romance.

One of the most striking examples of this tendency relates to the notion that native peoples, living in a state of primitive simplicity, enjoy free sexual relationships without shame or guilt. Aphra Behn's theme was taken up again 80 years later by John Cleland in a play entitled *Tombo-Chiqui or the American Savage*. Tombo-Chiqui is an American Indian brought to London by a young gallant who has deliberately kept him ignorant of European customs, in order to enjoy the spectacle of savagery confronted by civilisation:

> 'I had a notion it would divert me to observe pure simple nature working in him, in comparison with the laws, arts, and sciences amongst us. The contrast will doubtless be singular.'[30]

Tombo-Chiqui duly does what a noble savage is expected to do: he criticises the laws and customs of European society, like rank and private property, as useless and recommends nature as a sole guide in our affairs.[31] When he tries to 'make love... savage-fashion' with a woman whom he finds attractive he is told that such things are not done in civilised societies, and that it is necessary to go through certain procedures before enjoying sexual relationships:

> *TOMBO-CHIQUI:* And why? is not she at her own disposal in what may please herself, when the thing does no harm to anyone else?

---

[30] J. Cleland, *Tombo-Chiqui or the American Savage*, London: 1758, Act I, Scene I.

[31] This literary stereotype of the uncorrupted native who offers a profound critique of Western civilisation came to be known as an 'Adario', following the publication of the Baron de Lahontan's *New Voyages to North-America* in France in 1703. The Baron (1666-1715) constructed an imaginary conversation in which he depicted himself as trying unsuccessfully to defend European civilisation against the ridicule of a wise old Huron Indian called Adario who speaks of the Indians' love of liberty, equality and peaceful living. 'In short', the Baron concluded, 'the name of savages which we bestow upon them would fit ourselves better.' (Quoted in L. Donald, 'Liberty, Equality, Fraternity: Was the Indian Really Egalitarian?', in J. A. Clifton [ed.], *The Invented Indian: Cultural Fictions and Government Policies*, New Brunswick: Transaction Publishers, 1990, p.146.)

SYLVIA: No, it is forbidden.

TOMBO-CHIQUI: You are great fools, to forbid yourselves any pleasure, that nature does not forbid you.[32]

There is a certain poignancy about this bit of special pleading when we reflect that its author, John Cleland, had enjoyed a great success with his erotic novel *Memoirs of a Woman of Pleasure*, usually known as *Fanny Hill* (1748-9), but found himself regarded as beyond the pale of the respectable literary establishment as a result.[33] *Tombo-Chiqui* was never performed, although Cleland stated in a petulant preface that the reason the playhouses had not acted it was because it had never been offered to them in the first place.

It was not, in any case, an original work, being the English version of a popular French play of 1722 called *L'Arlequin Sauvage*, or *Harlequin the Savage*. Whilst there is a certain naïve charm about the simple critique which the play makes of hypocrisy and affectation, it is clear that it was not intended as a serious recommendation of the savage lifestyle. The noble savage here was simply a satirical literary device.

In the twentieth century, however, the savage who can be held up as an example to us all crossed over from the harlequinade to the supposedly more serious world of anthropology. In 1928 Margaret Mead published her book *Coming of Age in Samoa*, which rediscovered the noble savage in the South Sea Islands. Mead's Samoans were innocent souls, amongst whom such crimes as murder and rape were unknown. They were also sexually promiscuous without experiencing any sense of guilt. According to Mead, sexual relationships represented the principal pastime of the young, and marriage was delayed to allow as many years of this pleasant activity as possible.

These claims about Samoan sexuality turned the book into an instant classic, which figured on the reading lists of university courses for decades. Its influence was immense: it provided an

---

32 J. Cleland, *op.cit.*, Act I, Scene IV.

33 See T. L. Altherr, 'Tombo-Chiqui: Or, The American Savage: John Cleland's Noble Savage Satire', *American Indian Quarterly*, Fall 1985, pp.411-20.

important part of the intellectual underpinning of the sexual revolution of the 1960s, rather like the Kinsey Reports, which shared a similar degree of scientific objectivity.

In fact, Margaret Mead's book was a gigantic fraud. Not only was she wrong on every point, she was just about as wrong as it was possible to be. She had gone to the island with a case to prove and she was not the sort of woman to let facts stand in her way. She ignored all evidence, historical and contemporary, which contradicted her thesis. For example, the records show that murder and rape were common in Samoa; indeed, Samoa appears to have had one of the highest rates of rape in the world, and the whole account of Samoan sexuality was ludicrously wide of the mark. Far from being promiscuous Arcadians, the Samoan females lived in a culture which enforced a rigid code of virginity amongst unmarried adolescent girls. Nor was this attributable to Christian missionaries: in pre-Christian times violation of the code had been punishable by death.[34]

Mead had protected herself from this unwelcome knowledge by staying at the home of an American missionary and his family, where she was visited by her informants. Many of these were young people who delighted in misleading the gullible American visitor, egging each other on to tell her increasingly ridiculous stories which she could have easily falsified if she had shown even an elementary degree of scepticism. But, of course, the myth was too precious to Mead for that.

The most extraordinary part of this depressing story is that the book remained a best-selling classic long after the hoax had been exposed. Mead refused to make any alterations to later editions,[35] and indeed it was unnecessary to do so as there was no shortage of gullible academics prepared to take her view of Samoa as the true one.[36] When Derek Freeman, who had spent over six years

---

[34] D. Freeman, *Margaret Mead and Samoa: The Making and Unmaking of an Anthropological Myth*, Cambridge, MA: Harvard University Press, 1983; see also D. Freeman, *The Hoaxing of Margaret Mead: A Cause Célèbre of 20th Century Anthropology*, Cambridge, MA: Harvard University Press, 1992.

[35] See A. Flew, *Thinking About Social Thinking*, London: Fontana, 1991, p.17.

[36] The unwillingness of academics to give up on 'the gentle Tasaday' in the 1980s (see

in Samoa compared with Mead's five months, wrote the conclusive exposé of the whole saga[37] in 1983 he found himself under the most bitter attack. As Matt Ridley puts it, Freeman's fellow anthropologists 'reacted like a tribe whose cult had been attacked and shrine desecrated, vilifying Freeman in every conceivable way except by refuting him'.[38]

Citizen Savage

There is no name more closely associated with the myth of the noble savage than that of Jean-Jacques Rousseau (1712-78), to the extent that many people think he started the ball rolling. In fact, as we have seen, the tradition was almost two centuries old by the time he took it up, but he gave it a potent twist. Rousseau had little interest in witty satires on European sexual and social customs; he took the savage into the real-life world of revolutionary politics.

Rousseau's views on savage life, or the 'state of nature', which he contrasted unfavourably with the 'state of society', were contained in his famous *Discourse on the Origin of Inequality*. This began as a prize-winning essay in a competition set by the Dijon Academy of Letters in 1750. The question which entrants had to address was: 'Whether the rebirth of the sciences and arts has contributed to the improvement of morals'. Realising that most entrants would defend scientific progress, Rousseau decided to take the opposite line – that every development which took us further from the state of nature was in reality a loss of virtue.

Rousseau argued, at tremendous length, that man in a state of nature lives a life free of all cares. He experiences no wants other than 'food, a female and sleep',[39] all of which are easily gratified,

---

Chapter Five) shows how comfortable prejudice can make itself in the Senior Common Room.

[37] D. Freeman, *Margaret Mead and Samoa...*, *op.cit.*

[38] M. Ridley, *The Origins of Virtue*, London: Viking Penguin, 1996, p.257.

[39] J. J. Rousseau, 'A Discourse on a subject proposed by the Academy of Dijon: What is the Origin of Inequality among Men, and is it authorised by Natural Law?', 1755, trans. G. D. H. Cole in J. J. Rousseau, *The Social Contract and Discourses*, Everyman's Library, London: J.M. Dent, 1997, p.61.

so he suffers from no unsatisifed desires. He lives a solitary life, dependent on no one else and thus totally at liberty to please himself. Savages are amazingly healthy – 'troubled by hardly any disorders'[40] – and peaceable. Rousseau imagines his savage:

> '...wandering up and down the forests, without industry, without speech, and without home, an equal stranger to war and to all ties, neither standing in need of his fellow-creatures nor having any desire to hurt them, and perhaps even not distinguishing them one from another.'[41]

This was not just nonsense, it was nonsense on stilts,[42] but it won the prize. The essay made Rousseau famous throughout Europe and gave him the entrée to fashionable and intellectual society which he craved. However, it did not sell many copies: it became – and remains – one of those classics that everyone has heard of and almost no one has read. Examining it today, the reader who is not put off by its silliness will probably be defeated by its tedium. Rousseau makes his point over and over again, in a hectoring and opinionated tone that alienates the reader even as it invites his admiration. The adulation with which its publication was greeted is so hard to understand now that the critic Jules Lemaitre described it as 'one of the strongest proofs ever provided of human stupidity'.[43]

Perhaps the most striking characteristic of Rousseau's prize essay, which appears not to have been noticed by the judges, was its complete lack of originality. There is not a single strand in his account of the noble savage which he had not copied from Montaigne's essay *On the Cannibals*, published 170 years before.

---

[40] *Ibid.*, p.56: '...we are tempted to believe that, in following the history of civil society, we shall be telling also that of human sickness'.

[41] *Ibid.*, p.79.

[42] After reading the essay, Voltaire wrote to Rousseau: 'No one has ever used so much intelligence to persuade us to be stupid. After reading your book one feels that one ought to walk on all fours. Unfortunately during the last sixty years I have lost the habit.' (Quoted in K. Clark, *Civilisation: A Personal View*, London: BBC and John Murray, 1969, p.274.)

[43] Quoted in P. Johnson, 'Jean-Jacques Rousseau: "An Interesting Madman"', in *Intellectuals*, London: Weidenfeld and Nicholson, 1988, p.7.

The difference between Montaigne and Rousseau is not their subject matter, but their tone.

Montaigne is credited with inventing the essay as a literary form. He was elegant, urbane and light of touch. He enjoyed pursuing lines of intellectual inquiry to see where they might lead, and he took his reader along with him. Rousseau's approach was very different. If reading Montaigne is like discussing ideas with an old friend on a long walk, reading Rousseau is liked being harangued in the students' union bar by Dave Spart. He was the prototype of the arrogant intellectual, and Paul Johnson puts him at the top of the list in his book *Intellectuals*, describing Rousseau as:

> 'the first to combine all the salient characteristics of the modern Promethean: the assertion of his right to reject the existing order in its entirety; confidence in his capacity to refashion it from the bottom in accordance with principles of his own devising [and] belief that this could be achieved through the political process.'[44]

It was the political ramifications of Rousseau's essay which made it important. His title, after all, was *A Discourse on the Origin of Inequality* – not the subject set by the Dijon Academy, and requiring some ingenuity on his part to make it fit. Rousseau's interest in comparing savage with civilised man was to trace the development of inequality, and the concomitant loss of liberty, in society. In the most famous passage he attributes the start of the rot to the establishment of private property:

> 'The first man who, having enclosed a piece of ground, bethought himself of saying *This is mine,* and found people simple enough to believe him, was the real founder of civil society. From how many crimes, wars and murders, from how many horrors and misfortunes might not anyone have saved mankind, by pulling up the stakes, or filling up the ditch, and crying to his fellows, "Beware of listening to this impostor; you are undone if you once forget that the fruits of the earth belong to us all, and the earth itself to nobody".'[45]

---

[44] *Ibid.*, p.2.

[45] J. J. Rousseau, *op.cit.*, (1755), Part Two, p.84.

Private property was followed by laws to protect it, magistrates to carry out the laws, and kings to pass them. The happy independence of the savage, who wants for nothing as he knows of nothing he might want, is replaced by the master/slave relationship of ruler to ruled, which is the result of civil society, association and trade. Thus civilised man sinks into 'the last degree of inequality' which endures until:

> 'the government is ... dissolved by new revolutions...The popular insurrection that ends in the death or deposition of a Sultan is as lawful an act as those by which he disposed, the day before, of the lives and fortunes of his subjects.'[46]

If Rousseau had written 'King' instead of 'Sultan' he might have found himself in the Bastille, but his contemporaries knew what he meant. Liberty and equality were notions that were being taken extremely seriously by the French intellectuals of the last part of the eighteenth century, and these ideas were to have a cataclysmic political outcome.

Although Rousseau died more than ten years before the French Revolution he was regarded by the revolutionaries as their intellectual inspiration. 'There is a great dispute among their leaders', wrote Edmund Burke, 'which of them is the best resemblance of Rousseau... He is their standard figure of perfection.'[47] His ashes were re-interred in the Pantheon, and the president of the National Convention declared at the ceremony that: 'It is to Rousseau that is due the health-giving improvement that has transformed our morals, customs, laws, feelings and habits'.[48]

Thus did the noble savage make his entrance onto the world stage of *real-politik*, and it was a bloody one. Mrs Aphra Behn's satiric barbs against Christianity and John Cleland's jokes about sexual hypocrisy were as nothing to the impact of Rousseau's savage. Nor did the revolutions end in France. In his book *The Latin Americans*, Carlos Rangel blames the insidious myth of the

---

[46] *Ibid.*, pp.109, 114.

[47] Quoted in P. Johnson, *op.cit.*, p.2.

[48] *Ibid.*, p.3.

noble savage – 'the Red Robin Hood, the Don Quixote of Communism'[49] – for the revolutionary politics of modern Latin America, which has done so much to impede economic development.

In Search of a New Role

The noble savage has been used to make different points at different times, depending upon the concerns of the moment. He has been in the propaganda offensive for a variety of causes, from the French Revolution to the sexual revolution. Rousseau's attack on private property portrayed the savage as proto-communist, while the primitivist fantasies of unrestrained masculinity dreamed up by neurotics and neurasthenics like Nietzsche and D. H. Lawrence[50] went some way towards smoothing the path to power of fascist dictators.

The noble savage is no longer required to prop up some of the causes for which he has been conscripted in the past. For example, we no longer need to go to Samoa or Surinam to find young men and women who enjoy unregulated sexual relationships without any apparent sense of guilt. In recent years, however, the noble savage has turned green and appeared on the frontline of a very modern propaganda offensive.

---

[49] C. Rangel, *op.cit.*, p.16, quoting M. Lowy, *The Marxism of Che Guevara: Philosophy, Economics and Revolutionary Warfare*, New York: Monthly Review Press, 1973, p.7.

[50] In December 1923 D. H. Lawrence invited some friends to a famously unsuccessful dinner party at the Café Royal which went down in Lawrentian legend as 'The Last Supper'. He asked them to join him in founding a back-to-nature commune in New Mexico, but they were unenthusiastic. The incongruity between the gilded luxury of the Café Royal and the rather more simple lifestyle he was proposing seems to have escaped the 'prophet of love'.

2. The Noble Eco-Savage

'In the beginning, all the world was America.' [1]

JOHN LOCKE

Salad Days

The decade of the 1980s saw the emergence of the Green or environmental movement as one of the most potent forces shaping the public policy agenda. The concerns which it voiced were not new, and some of its constituent bodies had long and illustrious histories. For example, the animal welfare movement and the conservation movement in architecture were represented by organisations founded a hundred years or more ago. However, the Green movement acted as a focus, bringing together campaigning bodies which had previously acted separately, from holistic medicine and organic farming to anti-nuclear activists and population controllers.

It proved to be more than the sum of its parts. Greenery represented a world-view, held with the fervour of a religious faith by many of its disciples, that Western lifestyles, based on the industrial model of society, were unsustainable. The human race was seen as being out-of-step with the natural order and, in a sense, locked into a struggle to the death with the planet. Green pundits – including many famous and influential figures – warned that the damage which was being done to the environment in pursuit of profits and an ever-expanding supply of consumer goods would lead to a major environmental catastrophe in the near future. Either we would be forced back into the stone age by a total despoliation of the earth and the

---

[1] J. Locke, *An Essay Concerning the True and Original Extent and End of Civil Government* (Second Treatise of Civil Government), Chapter 5, para. 49, 1690.

destruction of its capacity to renew itself, or else we might be wiped off the face of the planet altogether.[2]

Politicians found themselves in a novel situation. Whereas previously they had come under attack if they had been unable to provide economic growth and rising living standards, they now found themselves vilified for doing just that. Greens demanded an end to economic growth and the idea that each generation can enjoy a higher standard of living than the previous one.[3] On the other hand, public support for environmental protection, as expressed through opinion polls, showed no sign of translating into a willingness to accept higher prices and lower living standards.

Trying to reconcile opposing demands, policy-makers developed the concept of 'sustainable development', arguing that economic growth is acceptable as long as we do not impair the capacity of the earth to support future generations. This concept was dismissed by leading Greens as 'a promise to carry on raping the Earth in as environmentally sensitive a manner as possible'.[4]

Greens continued to argue that the entire Western lifestyle was at fault, and that the problems could not be solved by tinkering with it at the margins. Western consumerism and industrialism were traced to the arrogance towards nature which was supposed to be the legacy of the Judeo-Christian tradition, in which man is seen as something apart from and superior to the rest of creation. Science itself was seen as an expression of this 'separateness'

---

[2] This view was summed up by James Lovelock, deviser of the famous Gaia hypothesis which sees the planet as a living and intelligent organism: 'If we think only of ourselves and degrade the earth, then it will respond by replacing humans with a more amenable species'. (J. Lovelock, 'Green science: an alliance for the coming world war', *The Sunday Times*, 1 October 1989.)

[3] Far from being a fringe view, this was taken up by such establishment figures as the Duke of Edinburgh: 'Economic growth cannot take place without making increasing demands on the ecology of the planet. The composition of that ecology can be changed, but it cannot be made to grow. It should be self-evident that attempts to maintain a constant rate of economic growth for more than a very limited time in a static ecology are doomed to failure.' ('The Future of the Countryside', *The Royal Society of Arts Journal*, Vol. CXXXVI, No. 5385, August 1998, p. 649.)

[4] D. Winner and J. Porritt, *The Coming of the Greens*, London: Fontana Paperbacks, 1988, p.72.

from nature: it allowed man to dominate and control the physical environment to such an extent that the very composition of the atmosphere was supposed to be critically affected.[5]

The only solution, according to the Greens, was a radical re-assessment of our lifestyle, and this in turn would involve a re-appraisal of our relationship with the rest of nature. We would have to 'redefine our relationship with the planet'. Fortunately, there were convenient role-models at hand. The native peoples of the earth were said to be living in the sort of harmonious relationship with nature which ensured minimal environmental damage. As the Green movement became more confident and demanding, so the promotion of the ecological wisdom of tribal peoples became more insistent:

> 'Green thinkers admire how tribal people live in harmony with their environment, taking care not to exhaust the land or use up the natural resources upon which they depend...'[6]

> 'Ancient people knew that they depended on the natural world for survival and had a close relationship with the forces of sky and earth...The people of ancient societies did not regard the human community as separate from the world of nature. The Earth was often seen as Mother, the giver and nourisher of life...'[7]

> '...all [indigenous cultures] consider the Earth like a parent and revere it accordingly...[They have] a perception, an awareness, that all of life – mountains, rivers, skies, animals, plants, insects, rocks, people – are inseparably connected. Material and spiritual worlds are woven together in one complex web, all living things imbued with a sacred meaning... According to indigenous law, humankind

---

[5] For the most famous and influential exposition of this point of view see L. White, 'The Historical Roots of our Ecologic Crisis', *Science*, Vol.155, No.3767, 10 March 1967, pp.1203-07.

[6] R. Kerven, *Saving Planet Earth*, New York: Franklin Watts, 1992, p.25.

[7] A. Pedersen, *The Kids' Environment Book*, Santa Fe, N.M.: John Muir, 1991, pp.12-13.

can never be more than a trustee of the land, with a collective responsibility to preserve it...'[8]

'The wisdom of the world's indigenous peoples is the accumulation of centuries of living not just *on* the land, but *with* it.'[9]

And so on, *ad nauseam* and *ad infinitum*. The wisdom of the tribal peoples, and its favourable contrast with the cruel rapacity of the white man's approach to the environment, has become one of the mantras of the Green movement. Primitive people, supposedly living in harmony with nature, have become, in Wallace Kaufman's phrase: 'the gold standard of the environmental movement. Against this standard it measures the values and achievements of our society'.[10] The environmental holocaust will only be averted, according to this argument, when we are humble enough to sit at the feet of tribal peoples and absorb their wisdom. As Richard D. North put it:

'In the neo-religion of the Greens, the tribal man and woman are Adam and Eve, their home is the Garden of Eden, and their state that which can obtain before the serpent of greed makes people eat the apple of industrial development.'[11]

The approach of the 1992 Quincentenary of Christopher Columbus's arrival in America brought the issue into sharp focus.

From Hero to Villain

In his book *1492 And All That*, Robert Royal considered the way in which attitudes towards Columbus and his achievements can be taken as a sort of barometer of America's opinion of itself.

---

8   J. Burger, *The Gaia Atlas of First Peoples*, Penguin, 1990, pp.21 and 23.

9   Paper bag, *Who Do We Think We Are?*, produced by The Body Shop.

10 W. Kaufman, *No Turning Back: Dismantling the Fantasies of Environmental Thinking*, New York: Basic Books, 1994, p.57.

11 R. D. North, *Life on a Modern Planet: A Manifesto for Progress*, Manchester: Manchester University Press, 1995, p.198.

For hundreds of years Columbus was viewed as an heroic explorer who had taken one of those giant steps for mankind. His bravery, daring and defiance of popular opinion had opened up half of the globe for conquest, commerce and investment. The riches of the Americas drew settlers who farmed, mined and exploited them. Christian missionaries preached the Gospel where it had never been heard before. Columbus became more than a national hero: he came to represent the very spirit of enterprise which was to make the USA into the richest and most powerful nation on earth.

By the end of the nineteenth century the reputation of Columbus had peaked. He had become 'the precursor of a confident and progressive United States of America', and the Columbian Exhibition in Chicago in 1893 'proclaimed 1492 not merely a historical date but a turning point in the emancipation of mankind'.[12] There was even a movement for his canonisation. Although the Vatican would not go so far, Pope Leo XIII issued an encyclical, *Quarto abeunte saeculo*, which praised Columbus in the highest terms:

> 'For the exploit is in itself the highest and grandest which any age has ever seen accomplished by man; and he who achieved it, for the greatness of mind and heart, can be compared to but few in the history of humanity.'

The Pope especially commended Columbus for bringing Christianity to 'a mighty multitude, cloaked in miserable darkness, given over to evil rites, and the superstitious worship of vain gods'.[13]

The mood of the 1992 Quincentenary was very different, and scarcely deserved to be termed a celebration at all. The achievements of Columbus had been re-assessed to put an entirely new slant on his actions. First of all, it was objected that he had not discovered America. There may have been other

---

[12] R. Royal, *1492 And All That: Political Manipulations of History*, Washington: Ethics and Public Policy Center, 1992, p.10.

[13] Quoted in R. Royal, *ibid.*, p.11.

24

explorers before him.[14] More importantly, the American Indians were not waiting to be discovered: they had been there for thousands of years. Columbus and the Europeans were accused of exploiting the Indians, of brutally mistreating and murdering them, of infecting them with European diseases to which they had no resistance, and of making them slaves in their own country. Christopher Columbus stood accused of genocide. According to Russell Means, a leader of the American Indian Movement, 'Columbus makes Hitler look like a juvenile delinquent', and asking Native Americans to celebrate Columbus Day was like asking Jews to appreciate a 'balanced view of the Holocaust' on Hitler Day.[15]

Even the churches failed to defend Columbus. The US National Council of Churches issued a statement on the quincentenary in which 'genocide was mentioned several times per page, while evangelization, in a positive sense, was not mentioned at all.'[16] One US Catholic Bishop even called on the Knights of St Columbus to change their name.[17]

Paradise Lost

The view that Columbus's arrival had not been an unmixed blessing for the native peoples of America was not entirely new: even at the 1892 celebrations there had been some protests by Indian organisations. However, the most characteristically modern note of the *furore* which surrounded the events of 1992 was the emphasis on the environment. Columbus had not only exploited the Indians, it was alleged, but he had been responsible for introducing into America an exploitative, European, Judeo-

---

14 Oscar Wilde used to say that those earlier explorers had been gentlemen who agreed to keep quiet about it.

15 Public statement on Friday 24 November 1989 outside the Florida Museum of Natural History's exhibition 'First Encounters: Spanish Explorations in the Caribbean and the United States, 1492-1570', quoted in R. Royal, *op. cit.,* p.19.

16 R. Royal, *ibid.,* p. 20, citing National Council of Churches in the USA, *A Faithful Response to the 500th Anniversary of the Arrival of Christopher Columbus*, resolution adopted by the Governing Board 17 May 1990.

17 *Ibid.,* citing D. Martinez, 'Bishop Challenges Knights to Drop Columbus', *National Catholic Reporter*, 25 August 1991.

Christian-based attitude towards nature which had led to the rape of the environment. This European ethic had crushed the Native American ethic of living in harmony with nature to the lasting detriment of both America and the planet. According to Winona LaDuke, a Native American, writing in the evangelical magazine *Sojourners*:

> 'The ecological agenda is what many indigenous peoples believe can, and must, unite all peoples in 1992. That agenda calls for everyone to take aggressive action to stop the destruction of the Earth, essentially to end the biological, technological, and ecological invasion/conquest that began with Columbus' ill-fated voyage 500 years ago.'[18]

This was not a fringe view. The October 1991 issue of *National Geographic,* entitled '1491: America Before Columbus', told its readers that Native Americans were closer to nature than we are now, living in a more harmonious relationship with their environment.

One of the strangest and most successful books to emerge from the 1992 Quincentenary was Kirkpatrick Sale's *The Conquest of Paradise.* As Robert Royal observes, the book is firmly within the noble savage tradition, which opposes noble savages (NSS) to savage Western civilisation (SWC), but Sale 'achieves a new high-water mark in the purity of his NSS and the utter blackness of his SWC'.[19]

Sale buys into the noble savage scenario so completely that he repeats the claim, derived from Montaigne and from Rousseau, that primitive peoples live lives free from disease. We can forgive writers who were working in the sixteenth and the eighteenth centuries for having little knowledge of cultures on the other side of the world, and for being too credulous of travellers' tales, but how can we account for the credulity of a modern author who believes that:

---

[18] W. LaDuke, 'We Are Still Here', *Sojourners*, Vol. 20, No. 8, October 1991, p.16, quoted in R. Royal, *op.cit.*, p.120.

[19] R. Royal, *op.cit.*, p.22.

'...to an extraordinary extent, the Americas were free of any serious pathogens...the Indians enjoyed remarkably good health, free of both endemic and epidemic scourges. As Henry Dobyns says... "People simply did not very often die from illnesses" before the Europeans came.'[20]

Surely Sale must have been thinking here of Shangri-La, or Neverland, rather than any location which could be found in an atlas? The conclusion which he reached, after several hundred pages of vilification of Columbus and the Europeans, was a dramatic call to his readers to become born-again environmentalists:

'There is only one way to live in America, and there can be only one way, and that is as Americans – the original Americans – for that is what the earth of America demands. We have tried for five centuries to resist that simple truth. We resist it further only at risk of the imperilment – worse, the likely destruction – of the earth.'[21]

As Robert Royal points out, Sale ridicules Columbus for entertaining medieval superstitions which led him to mistake the coast of Venezuela for the site of the Garden of Eden, but Sale himself is prey to some even more extraordinary modern superstitions. He 'predicts something very like the Last Judgement if we do not repent of our Western ways. Native American ways mirrored a perfect life in the Garden of Eden and point the way toward the New Jerusalem'.[22]

Unfortunately for Sale, and for others who see the adoption of traditional native attitudes towards the environment as the means of salvation, evidence has been mounting for some time that undermines the credibility of the notion of the noble eco-savage. It seems that native peoples may not always have lived by a conservationist ethic in the past, and that their modern descendents can still be just as destructive as the white man. We need to disentangle the myth from the reality.

---

[20] K. Sale, *The Conquest of Paradise: Christopher Columbus and the Columbian Legacy*, New York: Knopf, 1990, p.160, quoted in R. Royal, *op.cit.*, p.23.

[21] K. Sale, *op.cit.*, p.369, quoted in R. Royal, *op.cit.*, p.25.

[22] R. Royal, *op.cit.*, p.25.

3. History vs. Mythology

MRS. ALLONBY: *Savages seem to have quite the same views as cultured people on almost all subjects. They are excessively advanced.*

LADY HUNSTANTON: *What do they do?*

MRS. ALLONBY: *Apparently everything.*[1]

OSCAR WILDE

The Age of Innocence?

The view that American Indians lived in a state of harmony with nature is not confined to environmental activists like Kirkpatrick Sale.[2] Even a scholarly body like the Smithsonian Institution could claim in one of its publications on Christopher Columbus that:

> '...pre-Columbian America was still the First Eden, a pristine natural kingdom. The native people were transparent in the landscape, living as natural elements of the ecosphere. Their world, the New World of Columbus, was a world of barely perceptible human disturbance.'[3]

There is a great deal of wishful thinking behind such statements. In fact, they could scarcely be more inaccurate. There is now a very considerable body of serious academic research which

---

[1] *A Woman of No Importance*, Third Act, 1893.

[2] Sale is not a professional historian but the co-director of the E.F. Schumacher Society and founder of the New York Green Party.

[3] H. J. Viola and C. Margolis (eds.), *Seeds of Change: A Quincentennial Commemoration*, Washington: The Smithsonian Institution, 1991, p.226, quoted in W. M. Denevan, 'The Pristine Myth: The Landscape of the Americas in 1492', in K. W. Butzer (ed.), 'The Americas before and after 1492: Current Geographical Research', *Annals of the Association of American Geographers*, Vol. 82, No. 3, September 1992, p.370.

demonstrates conclusively that the Indians made a massive impact on their environment before the arrival of the white man, and that much of this impact was damaging and showed no conception of a conservation ethic. As William Denevan put it in a review of the research for the Association of American Geographers:

> 'By 1492 Indian activity throughout the Americas had modified forest extent and composition, created and expanded grasslands, and rearranged microrelief via countless artificial earthworks. Agricultural fields were common, as were houses and towns and roads and trails. All of these had local impacts on soil, microclimate, hydrology, and wildlife.'[4]

The view of the pre-Columbian Indians as noble eco-savages derives from two misconceptions. The *first* is that there were not many of them. The *second* is that they had no desire to modify the natural environment.

The Population Implosion

However, when Columbus arrived, America was not a sparsely populated continent. According to the Spanish priest Bartolomé de las Casas, who followed Columbus, the New World was 'full of people, like a hive of bees, so that it seems as though God had placed all, or the greater part, of the entire human race in these countries'.[5]

Denevan reviewed the population estimates for the period and came to the conclusion that the Indian population had amounted to 53.9 million, and that there were large populations not only in Mexico and the Andes, but even in the unattractive habitats such as the rainforests of Amazonia, the swamps of Mojos, and the deserts of Arizona.[6]

However, the arrival of the white man precipitated what was probably the worst demographic disaster in history. It was not

---

[4] W. M. Denevan, *op.cit.*, p.370.

[5] F. A. MacNutt, *Bartholomé de las Casas: His life, his apostolate, and his writings*, New York: Putnams, 1909, p.314, quoted in W. M. Denevan, *op.cit.*, p.370.

[6] *Ibid.*, pp.370 and 379.

warfare but disease which played the major part. The Indians had no resistance to tuberculosis, pneumonia, cholera, typhus, smallpox and other European ailments, with the result that their populations declined by about 90 per cent between 1492 and 1650, disappearing altogether in some areas. Although there was immigration of Europeans and Africans, this came nowhere near to replacing the lost numbers, with the result that by 1750 the population of the continent was still only about 30 per cent of that which had inhabited America at the time of Columbus's arrival.[7]

The effect of this population decline on the environment was dramatic. Large areas which had been intensively impacted by human activities reverted to a wild state. Fields and grasslands became forests, with the result that the poets and naturalists of the Romantic era gazed at trees which were less than 200 years old and spoke of the 'forest primeval', as if it has been there forever. As one commentator put it, 'the virgin forest was not encountered in the sixteenth and seventeenth centuries; it was invented in the late eighteenth and early nineteenth centuries'.[8]

The second misconception, that Indians had no desire to disturb nature, is even more wide of the mark. As historian Stephen Pyne has pointed out, they 'possessed both the tool and the will to use it. That tool was fire.'[9]

Making a Bonfire of the Forests

There is perhaps no sight more distressing to the modern environmentalist than a forest on fire. How many members have been recruited for campaigning bodies by those images of Amazonia ablaze? And how many times have we heard that such a destructive attitude towards the environment is the product of Western man's alienation from nature?

---

[7] *Ibid.*, p.371.

[8] S. J. Pyne, *Fire in America: A Cultural History of Wildland and Rural Fire*, Princeton, N.J.: Princeton University Press, 1982, pp.46-7.

[9] S. J. Pyne, *ibid.*, 1982, p.71, quoted in A. Chase, *Playing God in Yellowstone: The Destruction of America's First National Park*, Boston: Atlantic Monthly Press, 1986, p.93.

In spite of this, we now know that the American Indians were forest-burners *par excellence*. As a result, it was not the forests which impressed the early settlers but the absence of them.[10] Thomas Morton, a Puritan, wrote in 1637:

> '...the Savages are accustomed to set fire of the Country in all places where they come, and to burne it twize a year, vixe at the Spring, and the fall of the leafe. The reason that mooves them to doe so, is because it would other wise be a coppice wood, and the people would not be able in any wise to passe through the Country out of a beaten path.'[11]

To the Indians, trees had no value. As hunter-gatherers, the Indians had to get the trees out of the way, partly for the obvious reason that it is easier to hunt when you can see where you (and the prey) are going, but also because the mammals which the Indians wanted to hunt are not found in forests.

> 'As the forest spreads, trees, which lock up greater amounts of water, lower the water table, drying the soil; as the forests age, insects and diseases spread. Entropy overtakes nature and eventually, as the forest becomes a monoculture, the animal kingdom becomes one as well. The open savannah that once supported bison, elk, deer, antelope, beaver, bears, birds, and wolves, becomes the closed boreal forest inhabited by squirrels, ravens, and pine martens, but little else.'[12]

Once the forests have been burnt, however, and the land transformed to grasslands and savannah, these desirable species become available. The species which the Indians most wanted to hunt, like bison, moose, elk and deer, are found most easily in areas of recently burnt forest, which is why they burnt the forests over and over again.[13]

---

[10] 'Virgin America, rather than a place where a squirrel could swing from tree to tree from the Atlantic to the Mississippi without touching the ground, as some said, was a place, Pyne reported, "where it was nearly possible to drive a stagecoach from the eastern seaboard to Saint Louis without benefit of a cleared road"' (A. Chase, *op.cit.*, p.95 quoting S. J. Pyne, *op.cit.*).

[11] T. Morton, *New English Canaan: or, New Canaan*, 1637, rpt., New York: Arno Press, 1972, pp. 52-4, quoted in A. Chase, *op.cit.*, p.94.

[12] A. Chase, *op. cit.*, p.94.

[13] See W. M. Denevan, *op.cit.*, pp.372-73. If Alston Chase's view that 'the number of

We are accustomed, from endless Hollywood Westerns, to the idea that Indians sent smoke signals to each other by waving a blanket over a campfire. The reality was more dramatic: whilst the Indians regularly used fire to communicate with each other, they would scarcely have bothered with anything less than torching a hillside.[14] Lewis and Clark, the two anthropologists who made the first serious study of Native American lifestyles at the beginning of the nineteenth century, wrote that Indians in the Rocky Mountains would set trees alight 'as after-dinner entertainment; the huge trees would explode like Roman candles in the night'.[15]

In 1992, in the wake of the Earth Summit in Rio de Janeiro, B.L. Turner and Karl Butzer wrote an article for *Environment* in which they examined the extent to which evidence supports the view that the American Indians, prior to Columbus, lived in a state of minimal interference with nature. Their conclusions with regard to the forests of America are so startling – in the sense that they completely contradict the received wisdom – that they are reproduced here in full:

- Deforestation in the Americas was probably greater before the Columbian encounter than it was for several centuries thereafter.

- Many of the primeval forests that were supposedly encountered by the Europeans in 1492 and that remain today, including forests with the highest biodiversity, were not 'pristine' or 'virgin' but were the product of extensive use and modification by the Amerindians.

---

animal species in an ecosystem...peaks about twenty-five years after a fire' is correct, this raises the interesting question as to whether the much-desired goal of biodiversity might not be most effectively pursued by more frequent burning of the rainforests.

[14] See S. Budiansnky, *Nature's Keepers: The New Science of Nature Management*, London: Weidenfeld and Nicolson, 1995, p.107.

[15] *Ibid.*

- The scale of deforestation, or forest modification, in the American tropics has only recently begun to rival that undertaken prior to the Columbian encounter.[16]

It was the decimation of the Indian population which resulted in the re-appearance of the rainforest – that 'virgin forest' so beloved of environmental propagandists. However, as Denevan says, 'There are no virgin tropical forests today, nor were there in 1492'.[17]

When Conservation Does Not Make Sense

According to the myth of the noble eco-savage, indigenous peoples live in such a sympathetic relationship with the ecosystem that they kill only for their immediate needs, and never on a scale likely to drive species to extinction. One writer on conservation was claiming in the 1930s that each native hunter 'can tell at any time the number of animals which he can dispose of each year in his district without damaging his supply'.[18] This notion, that native peoples are prevented from depleting stocks of wildlife and other resources by some sort of cultural mechanism or religious belief, is based on the peculiar notion that they are not like other human beings, and do not respond to the same incentives and disincentives as the rest of us. However, for peoples living in the midst of abundant resources, in pre-market societies with poorly defined or non-existent institutions of private property, it made perfect sense to take as much as possible and move on. To leave possible targets un-hunted, on the assumption that they should be left for other hunters or future generations, would have seemed absurd. How

---

[16] B. L. Turner and K. W. Butzer, 'The Columbian Encounter and Land-Use Change', in *Environment*, Vol. 34, No. 8, October 1992, p.42.

[17] W. M. Denevan, *op.cit.*, p.375.

[18] W. C. McLeod, 'Conservation Among Primitive Peoples', *Scientific Monthly*, Vol. 43, 1936, p.565, quoted in C. E. Kay, 'Aboriginal Overkill: The Role of Native Americans in Structuring Western Ecosystems', *Human Nature*, Vol. 5, No. 4, 1994, p.379.

could they have known who would benefit from such altruistic behaviour?

The favourite Indian hunting device of the 'jump' illustrates this attitude. In order to kill as many buffalo as possible, with minimum risk to the hunters, herds would be stampeded over a cliff, so that the fall would kill them. In his book *Playing God in Yellowstone*, Alston Chase describes the effect of these jumps on species numbers:

'The Vore buffalo jump site in Wyoming...was used five times between 1550 and 1690, and holds remains of 20,000 buffalo. That means 4,000 or more buffalo were killed each time the jump was used. Other buffalo jumps in the West display the remains of as many as 300,000 buffalo. These sites were so numerous, in fact, and held such large deposits of bone, that for many years they were mined as a source of phosphorus for fertilizer!' [19]

These killing techniques were often so effective that large amounts of meat were left to rot and herds of animals were decimated, and sometimes driven to local extinction. Buffalo and antelope traps killed so many that it took the herds decades to recover. An average jump site was used only once or twice in a person's lifetime, but archaeologists surmise that it was the limitation of animal numbers, not Indian ingenuity or sense of self-restraint, that determined how often these jumps could be used. 'One successful kill of a number of adult animals,' wrote one commentator, describing the effects on the ecosystem of a jump near Jackson Hole, 'would have reduced the breeding potential of the local [bison] herd to a level where it was no longer a significant part of the valley ecosystem'.[20]

Extinction Is Forever

As Chase goes on to show, the American Indians were almost certainly responsible for the extinction of many large mammal species:

---

[19] A. Chase, *op. cit.*, p.99, citing G. C. Frison, *Prehistoric Hunters of the High Plains*, New York: Academic Press, 1978, pp.239-44.

[20] Quoted in A. Chase, *op.cit.*, p.100.

'Until ten thousand years ago an incredible bestiary of mammals roamed North America. These were the so-called mega-fauna, an exotic menagerie that included the woolly mammoth, saber-toothed tiger, giant sloth, giant beaver, camel, horse, two-toed horse, and dire wolf. These were the dominant fauna on this continent for tens of millions of years. Then suddenly and mysteriously they disappeared.'[21]

The disappearances cannot be accounted for by changes in climate or habitat, nor by theories of the survival of the fittest. Furthermore, it was only the mammals which vanished, usually more resilient than other species. The only explanation is that the Indians had hunted them to extinction.

The re-introduction into America, by the white man, of the horse, followed by the gun, made the remaining Indians even more of a threat to wildlife, in spite of their declining numbers. As they pursued quarry to the point of virtual extinction, the quality of the Indian diet first deteriorated, then began to approach starvation for some tribes.[22]

The Overkill Hypothesis

The historical record for the tribal peoples of other countries is not much more encouraging. When the Aborigines arrived in Australia the fauna 'included a large variety of monotremes and marsupials, including "giant" forms of macropodids (kangaroos and related species). Within 15,000 years all were extinct'.[23] The 'prime peoples' of Madagascar hunted several species of giant

---

[21] *Ibid.*, p.100.

[22] 'When Lewis and Clark first met the Shoshone in 1805, they were starving. Their chief told the explorers they had "nothing but berries to eat"...Another explorer, visiting the Lemhi...in 1811, described them as the "poorest and most miserable nation I ever beheld; having scarcely anything to subsist on except berries and a few fish"', (*Ibid.*, p.103.)

[23] M. S. Alvard, 'Conservation by Native Peoples: Prey Choice in a Depleted Habitat', *Human Nature*, Vol. 5, No. 2, 1994, p.130, citing J. Horton, 'Red Kangaroos: Last of the Australian Megafauna', in P. Martin and R. Klein (eds.), *Quaternary Extinctions*, Tuscon: University of Arizona Press, 1984, and P. Murray, 'Extinctions Down Under: A Bestiary of Extinct Australian Late Pleistocene Monotremes and Marsupials', in P. Martin and R. Klein, *op.cit.*

lemur to extinction,[24] while the arrival of the Maoris in New Zealand was quickly followed by the extinction of 34 species of birds.[25] As Matt Ridley puts it, 'the first Maoris sat down and ate their way through all twelve species of the giant moa birds', leaving about a third of the meat to rot, and entire ovens stuffed with roast haunches unopened, so plentiful was the initial supply.[26]

Peter Martin developed what has become known as the 'Overkill Hypothesis' to explain the disappearance of large numbers of species – particularly mammal species – over the relatively short time-span of a few thousand years following the arrival of humans on the different continents. He argued that, where animals had plenty of time to get used to humans, as in Europe and Africa where *homo sapiens* first appeared, they learned to be cautious. It was the arrival of man in Australia and America which was particularly devastating as the animals did not know what to expect and provided easy targets. North America lost 73 per cent of its large mammalian species, South America 79 per cent, Australia 86 per cent, but Africa only 14 per cent.[27]

It appears that most tribal peoples never worried about extinction, and probably had no concept of it. As Wallace Kaufman points out in *No Turning Back*, given the opportunity they would pursue any prey species in whatever numbers were available, and often for reasons which were quite as frivolous as any associated with modern consumerist societies. For example, '[s]ome of Hawaii's extinct birds ended up in beautiful feather

[24] *Ibid.*, citing R. Dewar, 'Extinctions in Madagascar: The Loss of the Subfossil Fauna', in P. Martin and R. Klein, *op.cit.*, and I. Tattersall, *The Primates of Madagascar*, New York: Columbia University Press, 1982.

[25] *Ibid.*, citing M. Trotter and B. McCulloch, 'Moas, Men and Middens', in P. Martin and R. Klein, *op.cit.*.

[26] M. Ridley, *The Origins of Virtue*, London: Viking, 1996, p.219.

[27] See P. Ward, *The End of Evolution: Dinosaurs, Mass Extinction and Biodiversity*, London: Weidenfeld and Nicolson, p.202.

capes',[28] some of which involved feathers from 80,000 birds.[29] Women of the Crow tribe of American Indians wore ceremonial dresses decorated with 700 elk teeth.[30] As only the two 'ivories' were used from each elk, this amounted to 350 animals per costume, which helps to put into perspective the famous Lynx campaign against fur coats which used the slogan: *It takes up to 40 dumb animals to make a fur coat but only one to wear it.*[31]

Sustainable Harvest?

An article in *People and the Planet*, the journal of the International Planned Parenthood Federation, described the challenge to the ecological wisdom of a tribe of Amazonian Indians presented by contact with modern economies:

> 'Cultural controls on over-exploitation, such as self-imposed restrictions on hunting certain animals or females during calving seasons... and protection of special groves of trees for religious reasons, have not been able to stand up to the seductions of the global market system.'[32]

This opposition of native wisdom to market forces is as familiar as it is wrong. In the cases where native peoples did practise sustainable use of resources it was because they had developed the institutions of private property and the market, often as a result of contact with white settlers.

---

[28] W. Kaufman, *No Turning Back: Dismantling the Fantasies of Environmental Thinking*, New York: Basic Books, 1994, p.65.

[29] Although it has been traditional to blame the arrival of Captain Cook in Hawaii in the eighteenth century for the extinction of so many species, we now know that between 80 and 90 per cent of the extinct bird species had vanished before then. (See P. Ward, *op. cit.*, pp. 232-38; and D. W. Steadman, 'Prehistoric Extinctions of Pacific Island Birds: Biodiversity Meets Zooarcheology', *Science*, Vol. 267, 1995, pp. 1123-31.)

[30] R. H. Lowie, *The Crow Indians*, Lincoln: University of Nebraska Press, 1935, quoted in A. Chase, *op.cit.*, p.99.

[31] Copy line by Bryn Jones to accompany a photograph by David Bailey, Lynx, c. 1986-7.

[32] J. McNeely, 'Diverse nature, diverse cultures', *People and the Planet*, Vol. 2, No. 3, London: International Planned Parenthood Federation, 1993, p.12.

The classic account of this is Harold Demsetz's 1967 essay on property rights[33] in which he describes the way in which the Montagne Indians of Labrador developed private property rights in beavers when they began trading with the settlers. Prior to the arrival of the white man, Indians had killed as many beavers as they wanted to eat and to clothe themselves. The beavers belonged to no one, so there was no mechanism to prevent over-hunting. The demand for and the value of the beaver pelts increased when settlers opened up lucrative markets with the white man, so the danger of over-hunting became more acute, just as it became more worthwhile to define property rights. To define and protect such rights consumes time and resources: no one will go to the bother of marking territories, patrolling boundaries and prosecuting trespassers unless the value of the resource being protected warrants the effort. When the Montagnes found they could make good money by supplying the furs that whites wanted to turn into coats they went to the trouble of establishing elaborate property rights with conservationist elements: each family would divide its hunting territory into quarters, hunting each quarter in rotation and leaving a 'protected' area in the middle which was not hunted at all except in emergencies.

Demsetz reinforced his theory by comparing Montagnes with the Indians of the southwest plains of America, who had very little by way of private property rights. He argues that this was attributable to the fact that these Indians hunted primarily grazing species, which wandered over very wide areas. These animals did not have the commercial value of the beavers, therefore the costs of establishing property rights would have been prohibitively high. It was more sensible to tolerate the risk of over-hunting.

As these examples show, the American Indians varied greatly in their customs and lifestyles, just as the peoples of Europe did. Terry Anderson has shown that some tribes had highly developed

---

[33] H. Demsetz, 'Toward a Theory of Property Rights', *American Economic Review*, Vol. 57, No. 2, 1967, pp.347-59. In this section of his article Demsetz draws heavily on the work of Eleanor Leacock: E. Leacock, 'The Montagnes' "Hunting Territory" and the Fur Trade', Memoir No. 78, *American Anthropologist*, Vol. 56, No. 5, Part 2.

systems of property rights, and that where their treatment of the environment was sustainable and conservationist, it was owing to the existence of these rights and not to any spiritual feelings towards nature.[34]

Not all American Indians lived as hunter-gatherers: many practised agriculture, sometimes on a very large scale and involving complex systems of irrigation. Once again, with the collapse of Indian populations throughout the Americas following the arrival of the white man, these farmed areas reverted to a wild state. Only in recent years have archaeologists uncovered the full extent to which Indian farmers affected their environment, particularly in central and southern parts of America. It appears that 'unsustainable' practices were to be found amongst the Indians who farmed as well as the Indians who hunted. Denevan speaks of:

> '...Central Mexico, where by 1519 food production pressures may have brought the Aztec civilization to the verge of collapse even without Spanish intervention. There is good evidence that severe soil erosion was already widespread, rather than just the result of subsequent European plowing, livestock, and deforestation.'[35]

Analysis of sediment in Lake Pátzcuaro in central Mexico found that, in the centuries preceding the arrival of the Spanish in 1521, soil erosion was occurring at extraordinarily high levels and that 'if anything there was a decrease in the erosion rate after the Conquest'.[36] The authors of this study warned against demands by environmentalists for a return to traditional forms of agriculture:

---

[34] 'Rather than promulgating myths that societies can solve their economic and social problems only by consciously choosing to revere and respect plant and animal communities, we should learn from American Indians that it is the institutional environment that matters most.' (T. L. Anderson, *Sovereign Nations or Reservations? An Economic History of American Indians*, San Francisco: Pacific Research Institute for Public Policy, 1995, p.xv.)

[35] W. M. Denevan, *op.cit.*, p.376, citing S. F. Cook and W. Borah, *Essays in Population History*, Berkeley: University of California Press, Vol. 3, 1971-79, pp.129-76.

[36] S. O'Hara, F. Alayne Street-Perrott and T. Burt, 'Accelerated soil erosion around a Mexican highland lake caused by prehispanic agriculture', *Nature*, Vol. 362, No. 48, 4 March 1993, p.49.

'As our findings indicate that traditional farming techniques cause significant erosion, it is unlikely that a return to prehispanic farming methods would solve the problem of environmental degradation'.[37]

How can we explain this destructive use of the environment, given the Indians' belief in the sacredness of nature, and the lack of any distinction between man and the rest of creation? Robert Royal argues that it was these very beliefs which contributed towards environmental destruction:

'When Indians wanted to cut trees, for example, they felt obligated to give the spirit to whom the trees belonged something in return, lest he grow angry and remove all trees. In many tribes the spirit was offered tobacco, and then the trees were cut.'[38]

In other words, the religious beliefs had no conservationist outcomes because the trees were cut just the same, and the tobacco made no difference to deforestation.

'In purely physical terms these religious practices could lead to great damage... [The Iroquois] broke off entire tops of trees to harvest cherries and, even before the white man's arrival, probably overhunted deer and beaver. Significantly, because of the way they exhausted resources, small native bands like the Iroquois had to move their villages approximately twice per generation.'[39]

Royal compares such tribes unfavourably with paper mill owners, who will replant forests purely out of self-interest. It is certainly true that the Indians believed (and believe) in a world filled with spirits, and viewed wildlife as their spiritual kin, but, as Charles Kay has argued in his paper 'Aboriginal Overkill', such kinship will not necessarily preserve animals in the absence of a scientific understanding of the environment:

---

[37] *Ibid*, p.50.

[38] R. Royal, *1492 And All That: Political Manipulations of History*, Washington: Ethics and Public Policy Research Center, 1992, p. 93.

[39] *Ibid*, citing W. N. Fenton, 'Northern Iroquoian Culture Patterns', in Vol. 15 of B. G. Trigger (ed.), *Handbook of North American Indians*, Washington: Smithsonian Institution Press, 1978, p. 298 and 302.

'Native Americans...believed that success in the hunt was obtained by following prescribed rituals and atonement after the kill. A scarcity of animals or hunting failures were not viewed as biological or ecological phenomena, but rather as a spiritual consequence of social events or circumstances. If a Native American could not find any game, it was not because he had overharvested the resource, but because he had done something to displease the gods. Since Native Americans saw no connection between their hunting and game numbers, their system of religious beliefs actually fostered the overexploitation of ungulate populations. Religious respect for animals does not equal conservation.'[40]

Kay argues that Native Americans had no conservation ethic, but rather 'acted in ways that maximized their individual fitness regardless of the impact on the environment'.[41] He illustrates his thesis by arguing from archaeological evidence that Native Americans hunted elk almost to extinction in the inter-mountain West, not only by slaughtering as many as possible at any given time, but by concentrating on killing the very animals whose deaths would have the maximum impact on the reproduction rate: prime-age animals, and particularly females. (Females were valued for their greater stores of fat and for their better hides.) This is the opposite of a conservation strategy.

Kay warns against confusing what people say they believe with what they actually do. To deduce from the knowledge that Native Americans professed kinship with nature that they were therefore good conservationists is like assuming that Christian nations must be peaceable and love their neighbours, because that is what is advocated by the Bible.

Environmentalist Him Speak with Forked Tongue

William Denevan concluded his exposé of the myth of the pristine wilderness by asking if it were possible that:

'...the thousands of years of human activity before Columbus created more change in the visible landscape than has occurred subsequently with European settlement and resource exploitation?

---

[40] C. E. Kay, 'Aboriginal Overkill: The Role of Native Americans in Structuring Western Ecosystems', *Human Nature*, Vol. 5, No. 4, 1994, p.379.

[41] *Ibid.*, p.359.

The answer is probably yes for most regions for the next 250 years or so, and for some regions right up to the present time.'[42]

Denevan's article, like others quoted in this chapter, was an overview. It was based on the work of dozens of scholars spread over decades. So how is it possible that the stereotype of the Native American as Noble Eco-savage has been so successfully promoted, without any reference to the corpus of research which contradicts this view? In their discussion of the American environment before and after Columbus, Turner and Butzer dryly observe:

'...the forests of the Americas, from Canada to Argentina, were so highly disturbed or modified by Amerindian use by 1492 that it is surprising that even the popular literature has missed this point.'[43]

Could it be that environmental campaigners missed this particular point because it suited their purpose to prolong the life of the noble savage myth? After all, if the aim of environmental activism is not just to tackle particular problems, but to present a nihilistic critique of modern, Western, growth-oriented market economies, then you need to offer an alternative model. The success of Kevin Costner's *Dances with Wolves*, whose saintly Indians were described by one reviewer as 'a mix of Timotei models and Relate therapists',[44] and of the Disney cartoon *Pocahontas*, with its nature-loving Indians and destructive British settlers, shows that there is a still a good deal of mileage left in the stereotypes.

Dances in Wolfshit

Finally, it would be remiss to conclude this historical account of the American Indian as noble savage without telling the story of Chief Seattle's speech. Claims that American Indians are natural conservationists are usually left unreferenced, as the Indians produced no literature. There is, however, one text which has

---

42 W. M. Devevan, *op.cit.*, p.381.

43 B. L. Turner and K. W. Butzer, *op.cit.*, p.37.

44 A. A. Gill, 'The plains truth', *The Sunday Times*, 28 May 1995.

become absolutely central to the propaganda offensive. This is a speech which was made by Chief Seattle, a chief of the Puget Sound tribes of the Pacific North West Coast of America, in 1854. It was made on the occasion of treaty negotiations which ceded a great deal of Indian land to white settlers, in return for certain promises of protection by the federal government.

Chief Seattle's speech has been quoted and published by environmentalist groups around the world as part of their campaign to persuade us that native peoples know something about protecting the environment which we do not. Here are some of the more frequently quoted passages:

'We are part of the earth and the earth is part of us. The fragrant flowers are our sisters. The deer, the horse, the great eagle, these are our brothers...The rivers are our brothers, they carry our canoes, and feed our children...The earth does not belong to us; we belong to the earth. All things are connected, like the blood which unites one family. Mankind did not weave the web of life. We are but one strand within it. Whatever we do to the earth, we do to ourselves.'

This all has a certain *naïf* charm, but as a historical document it has one significant drawback: it is completely bogus.

The version of Chief Seattle's speech which is now circulated by environmentalist and church groups was written by a scriptwriter called Ted Perry for a TV documentary produced by the Southern Baptist Radio and Television Commission, and broadcast in 1972. Perry claims that he had made it clear, in his original script, that he was creating a modern version of what Chief Seattle actually said, but that the programme was altered in a way that confused the issue. According to an account of *l'affaire Seattle* which appeared in *Reader's Digest*,[45] Perry tried to alert people to the modern nature of the text when he found that it was being promoted as an example of ancient tribal wisdom, but gave up when he realised that it had acquired a life of its own. The speech was turned into one of the most successful environmental books for children, *Brother Eagle, Sister Sky: A Message from Chief Seattle* by Susan Jeffers. It sold hundreds of thousands of copies in Britain and the USA, but when Perry

---

[45] M. Murray, 'Little Green Lie', *Reader's Digest*, August 1993.

wrote to the publisher pointing out that he was the author of the words quoted, he received a letter from their lawyers denying that there had been any infringement of copyright. No correction was made to the text of the book.

In fact the dubious nature of the text should have been obvious on internal evidence alone. At one point Perry had Seattle saying: 'What is there to life if you cannot hear the lonely cry of the whippoorwill?' What indeed, but it is unlikely that Seattle would ever have heard it, as the bird is not native to the Pacific North West. More notoriously, Perry has Seattle claiming:

> 'I have seen a thousand rotting buffaloes on the prairie, left by the white man who shot them from a passing train. I am a savage and do not understand how the smoking iron horse can be more important than the buffalo, which we kill only in order to stay alive.'

Once again, buffalo were not native to Puget Sound, and in any case the first transcontinental railways were not built until more than ten year after the date of the speech.

In fact we do have a reasonably good idea of what Chief Seattle said. A Dr Henry Smith, who was amongst his auditors, was so impressed by the Chief's words that he made detailed notes of the speech, which were later published. They contain none of the environmental references, and little that would be of use to modern activists, beyond an accusation that the white man can bury his ancestors and then move on, while such a burial site would always be sacred to the Indian. The text of the real speech is moving enough, and was not in need of embellishments in order to convey the impression of an imposing leader and orator. Seattle clearly understood the imbalance of power between the white man and the Indian: 'the red man no longer has rights that he [the white man] need respect'. However, he is not bitter about it and speaks optimistically of the promises of protection from 'Our great father Washington' (the Indians thought that George Washington was still alive), and of his hope that 'the hostilities between the red-man and his pale-face brothers may never return'.

In spite of the fact that *l'affaire Seattle* has been exposed in several scholarly and popular journals,[46] the environmentalists continue to use the 'speech' as a propaganda weapon. They clearly find it too useful a means of re-enforcing the stereotype of the American Indian as Noble Eco-Savage to give it up. Susan Jeffers defended the continued circulation of her book *Brother Eagle, Sister Sky*, by saying that: 'When you say someone is Native American, you can make certain assumptions about what he felt to be important.'[47]

This is the crux of the issue. As Ron Brunton pointed out in an article on Chief Seattle, the most important lessons to be drawn from the Seattle hoax are not primarily the creativity, gullibility and mendacity of the Greens and their allies in the media – anyone familiar with the movement takes those for granted – but the fact that: 'the ideas and emotions expressed in the speech are a product not of some American Indian culture, but of our own culture. They were written by an American author, for a Western audience'.[48]

In other words, they express an attitude towards the environment which is held by some Western environmentalists, but not necessarily by Native Americans or any of the other 'prime peoples' of the earth. Truly, Chief Seattle has been called the White Man's Indian, but he was not the first and will certainly not be the last. As Christian Feest has shown in his essay 'Europe's Indians', Europeans learned long ago how to project onto the Indians the qualities they were looking for in their own societies.[49] 'Hungarians show greater interest in the

---

[46] The first and most detailed account of the origins of the speech was by R. Kaiser, '"A Fifth Gospel, Almost", Chief Seattle's Speech(es): American Origins and European Reception', in C. F. Feest (ed.), *Indians and Europe: An Interdisciplinary Collection of Essays*, Aachen: Edition Herodot, 1987. For a good scholarly account see also P. S. Wilson, 'What Chief Seattle Said', *Environmental Law*, Vol. 22, pp.1,451-468.

[47] M. Murray, *op.cit.*, p.57.

[48] R. Brunton, 'Chief Seattle: White Man's Indian', *IPA Review*, Vol. 45, No. 2, 1992, pp.54-56.

[49] The gullibility of Westerners on the lookout for savage support for current fads guarantees a supply of frauds, some of which have been quite revealing. One hoaxer, calling himself Big Chief White Horse Eagle, toured Europe in the 1920s and 1930s

45

Indians' horsemanship, Germans in their military skills, and the French in making love to Indian maidens.'[50] However, these Westernised Indians all had one thing in common: they bore as much resemblance to the real American Indians as the 'Indian Chief' in Village People, who used to prance around in a feathered headdress singing the praises of the Young Men's Christian Association.

---

and made a big impression on museum curators and academics. The director of a museum in Vienna was convinced he must be a genuine Indian because he refused to shake hands with Jews. (C. F. Feest, 'Europe's Indians', in J. A. Clifton (ed.), *The Invented Indian: Cultural Fictions and Government Policies*, New Brunswick: Transaction Publishers, 1990, p.323.)

[50] C. F. Feest, *ibid.*, p.317.

4. Treading Lightly on the Earth

'I was prepared for the nobility of the Indians...but it was their pragmatism that knocked me sideways...The lessons they had to teach us were so self-evident that I was appalled that we hadn't already learned them.' [1]

ANITA RODDICK

Towards the end of the eighteenth century noble savagery was a favourite topic of the tea tables of fashionable London, largely owing to the success of Rousseau's essay.[2] There was great excitement, therefore, when, in 1775, a genuine savage called Omai arrived in town. He was brought from the newly-discovered Friendly Islands by Captain Fernaux in the Adventure, sister-ship to Captain Cook's Resolution. Omai was taken up by Lord Sandwich and paraded as a curiosity. He went to Cambridge and to Portsmouth (where he saw the ships), he shook hands with George III and was painted by Sir Joshua Reynolds. When society tired of him (as it inevitably would) he was sent back to his island, where he was said to have spent the rest of his life pining for the glorious sights he had seen in England.[3]

---

[1] A. Roddick, Introduction to D. Maybury-Lewis, *Millennium: Tribal Wisdom and the Modern World*, New York: Viking, 1992.

[2] Samuel Johnson was one of those who did not go along with the craze. Boswell has left us an account of his reaction to a man who summed up the contented lifestyle of the savage in the following words, which he clearly thought profound: 'Here am I, free and unrestrained, amidst the rude magnificence of nature, with this Indian woman by my side, and this gun, with which I can procure food when I want it: what more can be desired for human happiness?' JOHNSON: 'Do not allow yourself, Sir, to be imposed upon by such gross absurdity. It is sad stuff; it is brutish. If a bull could speak, he might as well exclaim - Here am I with this cow and this grass; what being can enjoy greater felicity?' (*Boswell's Life of Johnson*, ed. H. Morley, London: George Routledge and Sons, 1891, Vol. II, p.194.)

[3] The poet Cowper pictured his grief in *The Task*, published in 1785:
'Rude as thou art (for we returned thee rude

Omai's visit was only one in a long sequence of such exhibitions which began when Columbus took some Indians back to Spain to give King Ferdinand and Queen Isabella an idea of what their New World was like. Some of these visits have been more successful than others. The Micmac Indians have a tradition that one of their number was exhibited before the King of France and his court and required to demonstrate his hunting skills. After killing a deer, which had been penned for him:

> 'not only did he butcher and cook the meat but...he also ate it, and then defecated in front of the noble audience, therewith completing the nutritional cycle and registering his disgust about having been made a mere object of curiosity'.[4]

In 1989 the rock star Sting took another noble savage on a Grand Tour of Western capitals, with an outcome which was not dissimilar to the Micmac display. Sting and Chief Raoni, of the Brazilian tribe of Kayapo Indians, were campaigning against the construction of a hydro-electric dam in the Amazon which would have flooded large areas of rain forest and displaced tribal peoples. The project was being funded by the World Bank, so the critical thing was to get this source of funding withdrawn. The dam became the focal point of the whole Save the Rainforest movement, with Hollywood stars, church leaders and TV chat show hosts all throwing their weight behind the campaign. It succeeded in its aim: the World Bank announced the cancellation of funding and the whole project collapsed.

Meanwhile Sting had established the Rainforest Foundation, through which he could channel his fundraising and campaigning efforts. Like almost all Western environmentalists, Sting saw the conservationist lifestyles of the rainforest Indians as the key to preserving the forests. He petitioned the President of Brazil to establish an Indian reserve and in this, too, he was successful. In

---

And ignorant, except of outward show),
I cannot think thee yet so dull of heart
And spiritless, as never to regret
Sweets tasted here, and left so soon as known.'

[4] C. F. Feest, 'Europe's Indian's', in J. A. Clifton (ed.), *The Invented Indian: Cultural Fictions and Government Policies*, New Brunswick: Transaction Books, 1990, p.319.

1991 the Kayapo Indians were granted rights to a protected area of about 25,000 square miles, and Sting announced that this would end rampant logging and mining in the area. 'Brazil is setting an example for the world', he announced. 'Now we have to do all we can to help ensure the decisions become reality'.[5]

Kayapo Inc.

Unfortunately the reality was not quite what Sting expected. It soon became clear that there was little the white man could teach the Kayapo Indians about logging and mining concessions. Chiefs began cutting deals which resulted in the extraction of reserves on a massive scale. In one village, Pukanav, the scale of logging was so great that 60 miles of new roads had to be built to get the timber out. When some of the timber was seized by environmental protection officers, the Pukanav chiefs made four flights – paid for by the logging company – to persuade the authorities to release it.[6] To be fair to the Kayapo, they had not waited for the protected area to be established for them by the government before starting their exploitive activities. In 1988 mahogany sales alone had brought them in $33 million, and this had been going on throughout the decade. Unfortunately, the benefits seemed to be experienced mainly by the chiefs and their families, who acquired houses, cars and planes. Meanwhile their villagers were without basic medical care. As *The Economist* pointed out, in 1988 the village of Kikretum received $1 million for timber and mineral rights, but still had a quarter of its children die in infancy.[7] When the Brazilian government, nervous of the disapproval of Western environmentalists, tried to get the Kayapo to stop deforesting the Amazon, the Indians protested in Brasilia and demanded compensation for lost revenues of $50,000 per village per month. 'The government, which is broke,

5   T. Moore, 'Rainforest Victory for Sting', *The Daily Telegraph*, 29 November 1991.

6   M. Moffett, 'Kayapo Indians Lose "Green" Image Amid Lure of Profit', *Wall Street Journal*, 29 December 1994.

7   'The savage can also be ignoble', *The Economist*, 12 June 1993.

would not pay; the Kayapo's trees continue to fall.'[8] Not for nothing had the Indians acquired the name of Kayapo Inc.

By this time Sting had withdrawn from the fray, expressing disillusion with the Indians:

> 'They're always trying to deceive you. They see the white man only as a good source of earning money, and then as a friend. I was very naive and thought I could save the world selling T-shirts for the Indian cause. In reality, I did little.'[9]

Disappointed Expectations

Sting's disillusion with the rainforest Indians was the result of unrealistic expectations that they would behave like the noble savages of legend, living in harmony with nature. Such legends have acquired a life of their own, often with unfortunate results. Measures designed to conserve populations of fish and animals are often suspended with regard to American Indians, on the assumption that they are unnecessary. For example, Indians can use gillnets which are banned for other fishermen in the Great Lakes, and the 'closed-season' on walruses and polar bears in Alaska does not apply to them. Terry Anderson[10] has written of the perverse outcomes of such measures:

- Major runs of salmon on the American West Coast have been wiped out by Indian gillnetting.

- On most western reservations big game populations have been brought to the verge of local extinction.

- Shoshones and Arapahos have almost wiped out elk, deer, moose and bighorns on the 2.2 million-acre Win River Reservations in Wyoming.

---

[8] *Ibid.*

[9] S. O'Shea, 'Bitter Sting learns laws of the jungle', *The West Australian*, 3 May 1993.

[10] T. L. Anderson, *Conservation Native American Style*, Bozeman, Montana: Political Economy Research Centre, PERC Policy Series No. 6, July 1996, pp.16-17.

Despite these failures, which have been well documented, the image of native peoples as natural conservationists is pervasive amongst policy-makers. The International Union for the Conservation of Nature and Natural Resources (IUCN) has set up a task force on traditional lifestyles which investigates the ways in which native peoples react with their environments, but the investigations are based on a definition of a traditional lifestyle as constituting: 'the ways of life (cultures) of indigenous people that have evolved locally and are based on *sustainable* use of local resources' (emphasis added). As Michael Alvard has argued in his article 'Conservation by Native Peoples', this is presuming what ought to be demonstrated.[11] The transfer of property rights can be rationalised on a number of grounds, including natural justice and restitution for past wrongdoing, but if such transfers are to be made with reference to the impact of native peoples on the ecosystem, we at least ought to examine the evidence to see how this is more 'sustainable' than anyone else's impact.

Empirical Evidence and the Piro

Alvard questions the assumption that native peoples are natural conservationists, using detailed studies which he and others have carried out on the Piro, a tribe of hunter/gatherer/farmers in the rainforests of south-eastern Peru. The most important species for the supply of meat to the Piro are ungulates (creatures with hooves) such as the Brazilian tapir, the collared peccary and the red brocket deer. After observing hunts for the best part of a year Alvard came to the conclusion that the Piro had no strategy of conservation, but on the contrary killed whatever and wherever they could. The areas closer to the village were, not unexpectedly, less fruitful hunting grounds than those areas of the forest farther away. It would have made sense, from a conservation point of view, to stop killing animals altogether in these depleted areas, in order to allow populations to revive. On the contrary, however, animals 'were pursued at almost every opportunity, even though such species as the large primates and

[11] M. S. Alvard, 'Conservation by Native Peoples: Prey Choice in a Depleted Habitat', *Human Nature*, Vol. 5, No. 2, 1994, p.147.

tapir have been identified as particularly vulnerable to local extinction'. [12]

Alvard believes that the misconceived view of tribal peoples as conservationists results from a misunderstanding of conservation. He defines behaviour as conservationist when 'a short-term cost is paid by the resource harvester in exchange for long-term benefits in the form of sustainable harvests.'[13] If a small number of tribal people are foraging in a vast area of land, they can exploit the environment without causing any long-term damage. It does not matter if they have no conservationist ethic, for example, as long as the animals can breed faster than the hunters are killing them. However, if the population of the tribal peoples grows, and the land available to them shrinks, then unsustainable treatment of the environment becomes both more damaging and more obvious.

In a chapter for the book *Tall Green Tales*, Ron Brunton gives an example of tribal people who practise an unsustainable and polluting lifestyle without making any major impact on the environment, except at a local level, owing to their small numbers. The Semang of the Malaysian peninsula disrupt the rivers by poisoning fish and by their toilet habits, they cause extensive damage to forest plants in the process of harvesting their products, and they have extremely high levels of air pollution in their villages as a result of domestic fires:

> 'If citizens of Malaysia's capital city of Kuala Lumpur were confronted with air pollution of the intensity normal in Semang households, they would rise up in outrage over the terrible state of the city's environment, and they would blame it on modernisation and capitalist industrialisation.'[14]

---

[12] *Ibid.*, p.143.

[13] *Ibid.*, p.127.

[14] A. T. Rambo, *Primitive Polluters: Semang Impact on the Malaysian Tropical Rain Forest System*, Anthropological Papers, University of Michigan, 1985, p.79, cited in R. Brunton, 'Indigenous people live in harmony with nature and have much to teach us about environmental stewardship', in J. Bennet (ed.) *Tall Green Tales*, Melbourne: Institute of Public Affairs, 1995, p. 4.

Brunton argues that attempts to force the Australian Aborigines into the mould of the noble eco-savage are equally misguided. He quotes Christopher Anderson, who wrote that environmentalists:

'...who are involved in dealings with Aboriginal people in conservation matters will become quickly disillusioned. One has only to camp in the bush with Aboriginal people in many areas and see children cutting down any and everything in sight to appreciate this.'[15]

Only Slaves Climb Trees

Allyn MacLean Stearman provided another example of indigenous people being profligate with their natural resources in her paper 'Only Slaves Climb Trees'.[16] She argues that some tribal peoples have developed conservationist habits, particularly when difficult environmental circumstances and shortage of resources have made this absolutely necessary for survival. It is not, however, possible to generalise, since groups living in the midst of plenty can be extremely wasteful of resources.

Stearman illustrates her argument with her own researches among the Yuqui Indians, who live in the humid tropical forests of eastern Bolivia. They behave in the very opposite way to anything which might be described as a conservationist ethic. When hunting they pursue whatever is available, without regard to age or sex of the prey. Pregnant females and females with young are particularly targeted because they are slow, and therefore easier to catch.[17] Fetuses taken from pregnant females are regarded as a delicacy. Fishing is aided by the use of Barbasco, which is deployed in such quantities that 'all the fish

---

[15] *Ibid.*, pp. 2-3, quoting C. Anderson, 'Aborigines and Conservationism: the Daintree-Bloomfield Road', *Australian Journal of Social Issues*, Vol. 24, 1989, p.220.

[16] A. M. Stearman, 'Only Slaves Climb Trees', *Human Nature*, Vol. 5, No. 4, pp.339-57.

[17] Archaeological evidence suggests a preference on behalf of aboriginal hunters throughout the world for prime-age females, which are prized on account of their higher fat content and hides which are less likely to be scarred from fighting. (See S. Budiansky, *Nature's Keepers: The New Science of Nature Management*, London: Weidenfeld and Nicholson, 1995, p.149.)

of even the larger lakes are taken without regard to protecting fry or seasonality of breeding. The stupefied fish, regardless of size, are simply scooped up in baskets.'[18]

Yuqui society was traditionally divided into masters and slaves, but contact with Westerners convinced the slaves that they did not have to be slaves any more. They set up households on their own, leaving their former masters to fend for themselves. One of the tasks which the slaves had performed was to climb fruit trees and throw down fruit to their masters. With no slaves to perform this menial task, the Yuqui have taken to gathering fruit by cutting down the trees. They justify this unsustainable behaviour by pointing out that 'only slaves climb trees'. The results are obvious. Some species of fruit tree have become almost extinct around Yuqui settlements, a fact which the Yuqui only seem to regret because it means they have to travel further to get their fruit. Missionaries attempted to persuade the Yuqui to plant trees and harvest the fruit, but the scheme broke down because as soon as a tree began to bear fruit, someone would cut in down. This led to bitter disputes between the planters and the cutters.

The fact that the Yuqui are not behaving in the manner expected of noble eco-savages by environmentalists has led to consequences far more serious than a shortage of fruit. In 1992 the Bolivian government gave the Yuqui rights over 115,000 hectares of land. Following a general election, the government became less sympathetic to the claims of indigenous people and suggested that these land rights might be revoked. Part of the rationale for this change in policy was the failure of the Indians to behave as the natural conservationists which environmental groups had made them out to be.

The Kayapo Indians experienced a similar backlash when they disappointed their environmental patrons. 'What the Kayapo are doing is absurd, illegal, immoral and wrong' was a typical

---

[18] Stearman, *op.cit.*, p.349.

comment,[19] although their behaviour was not so very different from that of other groups of Brazilian entrepreneurs. Once again there is a growing political movement in Brazil to curtail Indian land rights and to make it more difficult to give legal status to Indian territories.[20]

We can thus see that the stereotype of the noble savage, conceived as a stick with which to beat the white man, can have negative consequences for the very people it is supposed to benefit. Tribal peoples soon find out that, if they fail to live up to their reputation for living transparently in the environment, treading lightly on the earth and so on, then environmentalists can be as ruthless in imposing their world-view as the *conquistadors* at their most imperialistic.

A Serious Case of Entrapment

Of all the areas in which the environmentalist's ideal of native lifestyles comes into conflict with the reality, there is no more inflammable flashpoint than the fur trade.

As we have already said, the Green movement which emerged in the 1980s represented an amalgamation of numerous pressure-group causes which had previously campaigned separately. One of the largest groupings within the new movement consisted of animal rights campaigners, most of whom were fundamentally opposed to the wearing of fur coats. The Green movement has produced no more powerful images than the world-famous photograph of the mother seal sniffing the bloody corpse of her recently-skinned pup, and the David Bailey cinema advertisement which showed a decadent audience being sprayed with blood which streamed from between the pelts of a fur coat, worn by a catwalk model.

---

[19] J. Epstein, 'Brazil Indians Defend the Sale of Gold, Trees: Ecologists, Politicians Criticize Practice', *The Dallas Morning News*, 6 November 1993, p.A20, quoted in A. M. Stearman, *op. cit.*, p.352.

[20] 'We are losing sight of the important fact that indigenous peoples have a basic human right to a home territory regardless of how they manage this land...These rights, however, cannot be contingent on some imprecise or even fallacious notion of the ecologically noble savage.' A. M. Stearman, *op.cit.*, pp.352-53.

As far as the anti-fur lobby was concerned, these luxury items represented a cruel and barbarous attitude towards the animal kingdom, and as long as the targets of their campaign could be presented as the super-rich, like the patrons of Harrods fur department, then the moral dimension of the issue remained relatively uncomplicated. There was, however, more to it than that because, while many fur pelts are produced by fur farmers in developed nations, there are also many which emanate from the lands of those very native peoples whom the Greens are promoting as the ideal stewards of nature. This posed a serious dilemma. How could the lifestyles of these 'prime peoples' of the earth be held up for emulation if they involved killing lots of furry animals?

The impact of the bloody seal photo was immediate. The seal-pelt trade came to a virtual dead halt,[21] depriving thousands of Inuit Indians of their livelihood. In 1989 *The Sunday Times* ran a report by Stuart Wavell on the effects of the ban:

> 'Last year, accompanying a judge's court through Inuit settlements along the Arctic cost, one could see the stark results of anti-sealing campaigns which had unintentionally enmeshed native people in an epidemic of alcohol-related crimes, stabbings, domestic violence and rape. Yet not long ago Eskimos were universally admired as industrious, cheerful folk who had forged a spiritual contract with animals.'[22]

By 1983 the native peoples had begun to fight back, challenging Western environmentalists to come and see the damage they had done to native communities. 'These people are so ignorant, so arrogant, so patronising, so stupid,' said an Inuit spokesperson. 'They know nothing about aboriginal people.' It was, as one journalist put it, 'a Leftist activist's worst nightmare: a traditionally oppressed group – whose endorsement is vital not only to your external legitimacy but also to your confidence in

---

21 'Between 1980-81 and 1987-88 the number of seal pelts exported annually from Canada's Northwest Territories fell by 97 per cent.' (P. Beinart, 'The Fur Flies', *The New Republic*, 13 December 1995.)

22 S. Wavell, 'Getting under furriers' skins', *The Sunday Times*, 5 November 1989.

the justness of your cause – allies with your opponents and skewers you with your own rhetoric'.[23]

In 1985 a Greenpeace spokesman told the Inuit: 'You have every right to be very angry with us. We will try to make sure this sort of thing does not happen again.'[24] However, by this time there was real tension within Greenpeace, where its principal anti-fur agitator, Mark Glover, was leading a campaign for action against trapping for wild furs. As more than 90 per cent of the four million wild fur pelts collected annually in Canada were caught by trapping,[25] and as 80 per cent of these were caught by native people, any such action would have had the effect of destroying the inland communities of Indians as certainly as the decimation of the seal-pelt trade had destroyed that of the coastal Indians. Branches of Greenpeace International began to distance themselves from the anti-trapping campaign, which was being run by Glover from the London office, but he was unrepentant. 'We are not an organisation that defends native people. We defend the environment', he was quoted as saying in *The Guardian*.[26] Glover then left Greenpeace to set up Lynx 'to discourage the use of fur by education and persuasion'.

In 1992 Lynx published a booklet called *Cruelty and Christian Conscience*[27] which contained a declaration signed by 41 Anglican bishops to the effect that they would never buy or wear fur. When it was pointed out to Philip Goodrich, the Bishop of Worcester, that the bishops wear fur-trimmed robes at the opening of parliament he replied: 'I hadn't thought of that... What a humbug I am.'[28] More seriously, the bishops received a

---

23 P. Beinart, *op.cit.*

24 Alan Pickaver, Greenpeace spokesman, quoted in P. Beinart, *op.cit.*

25 J. Best, 'Animal rights campaign: Canada fur trade under fire', *The Times*, 22 December 1986.

26 S. Wavell, 'Greenpeace at war with itself', *The Guardian*, 8 June 1985.

27 A. Linzey (ed.), *Cruelty and Christian Conscience: Bishops Say No To Fur*, Nottingham: Lynx, 1992. The front cover of the booklet showed otters and foxes being taken up into heaven by cherubs.

28 D. Thompson, 'Bishops denounce fur trade', *The Daily Telegraph*, 24 November 1992.

letter signed jointly by the Primate of the Anglican Church in Canada and the Bishop of Saskatchewan warning that 'The current anti-fur campaign by Lynx threatens the aboriginal peoples and their way of life [and] violates the dignity of aboriginal peoples and their traditions'.[29] Following representations by Chief Bill Erasmus of the Dene nation, together with representatives of the Micmac and Cree tribes, David Hope, the Bishop of London, said: 'I signed the document because I felt that Lynx had made a compelling case. However, the Indians' views were not part of that case, which makes me think we need to take another look at the question.'[30]

To expose the confusion of these be-furred bishops is, as Oscar Wilde would have said, more than a duty: it is an absolute pleasure. However, their dilemma is symbolic of the muddle people get themselves into when they trade in sentimental images of native people. As Alston Chase put it: 'Hunter-gatherers... were attractive to white people only so long as they were no longer hunting or gathering.'[31] It is impossible to square reverence for native lifestyles with the requirement that these should conform to the prejudices of lobbyists in London. If the lifestyles are admirable and worthy of imitation, then they have to be accepted for what they are, killing and all. On the other hand, if we intend to turn the native peoples of the earth into characters in the world's largest theme parks, where they can act out the fantasies of Western eco-freaks, then perhaps we should issue them with mouse-ears right away and have done with it.

---

[29] Bishop Michael Marshall, 'All this and a decade of evangelism too!', *Church of England Newspaper*, 5 March 1993.

[30] D. Thompson and B. Fenton, 'Indian chief takes bishops to task over fur boycott', *The Daily Telegraph*, 16 February 1993.

[31] A. Chase, *Playing God in Yellowstone: The Destruction of America's First National Park*, Boston: Atlantic Monthly Press, 1986, p.113.

5. From Arcadia to Utopia

'A map of the world that does not contain Utopia is not worth even glancing at.' [1]

OSCAR WILDE

'One or Two People Want to Go There'

There is an ancient literary tradition, going back at least to Plato's *Republic*, of constructing imaginary ideal societies. Such attempts include Francis Bacon's *New Atlantis* (1626), Jonathan Swift's *Gulliver's Travels* (1726), Samuel Butler's *Erewhon* (1872), William Morris's *News From Nowhere* (1890), and H. G. Wells's *The Time Machine* (1895).[2] The creators of these happy communities usually had some particular axe of their own to grind by way of a solution to society's problems: for William Morris the answer was socialism, in Samuel Gott's *New Jerusalem* (1648) it was education, and in Campanella's *City of the Sun* (1623) it was eugenics.[3]

By far the most famous example of the *genre* is Thomas More's *Utopia*, which has given its name to the concept of a perfect society where life is without care. It was published in 1516, in the same year as Peter Martyr's book *De Orbe Novo*, which purported to give an account of the lifestyles of the Brazilian Indians, as related by the Spanish explorers of the New World. The Indians were depicted as living in a state of bliss,

---

[1] *The Soul of Man under Socialism*, 1891.

[2] For a discussion of Utopia and its sequels see N. Dennis and A. H. Halsey, *English Ethical Socialism: Thomas More to R. H. Tawney*, Oxford: Clarendon Press, 1988, p.18.

[3] For further discussion of literary utopias see P. Turner (trans.), Thomas More's *Utopia*, Harmondsworth: Penguin, 1965, editor's introduction, p.19. See also G. Claeys (ed.), *Modern British Utopias 1700-1850*, London: Pickering and Chatto, 1997.

with no need for private property as the land was so abundantly fertile. More incorporated this element into his book. His Utopians are free of the encumbrance of private property: they eat at no charge in communal dining halls and simply ask for anything they want in the shops. No one asks for more than they want because there would be no point in hoarding: everything is free anyway.

More took good care, however, that his readers should not be misled by his fantasy. He made an elaborate joke in his prefatory material about the way in which, whilst he and his friend were listening spellbound to the tale being spun about Utopia by the traveller Raphael, they both forgot to ask him where it was. 'It makes me feel rather a fool...not to know what sea it's in...there are one or two people in England who want to go there.'[4]

In fact, Utopia is Greek for No-place.[5] *Pace* Oscar Wilde, it is not to be found on any map, but that has not stopped a number of determined explorers from looking for it.

Gold Fever

In 1595 Sir Walter Raleigh set out for 'that mighty, rich and beautiful empire of Guiana, and... that great and golden city which the Spaniards call El Dorado'.[6] Raleigh was a hard-headed – some would say unscrupulous – adventurer, and yet he undertook a long, dangerous and expensive journey to modern-day Venezuela because he thought that he would find El Dorado, the legendary city of gold, lost and overgrown in the jungle. His chief backers, Charles Howard, the Lord Admiral, and Sir Robert Cecil, were skilled operators of the first rank in the ruthless world of Elizabethan politics, and yet they put up – together with a few others – £60,000 (£25 million in today's money) for this crazy scheme. They seriously expected a return on this investment in a voyage to fairyland.

---

[4] P. Turner, *ibid.*, p.31.

[5] There is a possible pun in the name, which could also mean Good Place.

[6] Raleigh's *Works*, ed. Thomas Birch, 1751, Vol. ii, p.141.

As Charles Nicholl has shown in his history of the adventure, *The Creature in the Map*, even these hard-headed men of affairs could not help being influenced in their business decisions by the stories of peace-loving Indians, living in the natural abundance of a golden age, which had been percolating back to Europe since the arrival of Columbus in America over a hundred years before.[7] By giving credence to such fantasies, the projectors of the El Dorado scheme were like 'people stepping through a frame, into a picture they have themselves created'.[8]

The results were predictably disastrous. Raleigh's difficult navigation of the Orinoco river into the Guiana Highlands was finally cut short by the rapids at the confluence with the Caroni river. He had to turn back, and returned to England with virtually nothing to show for it all. Many of his men were dead. His backers lost money and he lost face, although curiously he never lost hope. Like so many other travellers in search of marvellous places, he was always convinced that El Dorado was there somewhere, around the next bend in the river, across the next range of mountains. In 1616, after spending 13 years in the Tower of London on charges of conspiracy, Raleigh was able to persuade an unsympathetic James I to allow him to make a second trip. There were two conditions: there must be no trouble with the Spanish, with whom the King wished for peaceful relations, and this time there had to be lots of gold. Raleigh failed on both counts, and when he returned a second time empty-handed he was tried and executed for treason.

The irony is that the legend was based on fact: the gold was there, not in the form of a lost city, but in the ground – where it

---

[7] Raleigh's view of the American Indians was coloured by reports he had received from his scout, Arthur Barlowe, on the condition of the native inhabitants of Virginia some years before. According to Barlowe, the people were 'most gentle, loving and faithful, void of all guile and treason, and such as live after the manner of the Golden Age'. The land was said to produce 'incredible abundance' and to smell 'so sweet and strong…as if we had been in the midst of some delicate garden'. (See D. B. Quinn, *Raleigh and the British Empire*, London, 1947, pp.91-116, quoted in C. Nicholl, *The Creature in the Map: A Journey to El Dorado*, London: Jonathan Cape, 1995, pp.301-02.)

[8] C. Nicholl, *ibid.*, p.20.

usually is. 'For a few years – until the discovery of the Rand goldfields in South Africa in 1886 – Venezuela was the biggest gold-producer in the world.'[9] It is still an important player, with almost all of the gold coming from the foothills of the Guiana Highlands, where Raleigh had been looking. He had seen some of the deposits but, apart from extracting a few samples with their daggers, his men could do little as they had taken no mining tools with them. They had seriously expected to find the precious metal in the more accessible forms of plated palaces with bulging treasuries.

'The dream of Sir Walter Raleigh concerning...Eldorado, may satisfy us, that even wise men are not always exempt from such strange delusions', wrote the economist Adam Smith two hundred years later.[10] At least Raleigh had the excuse that geography was in its infancy, when gaps in the atlas could be filled in with monsters and mermaids. But what are we to say of modern fantasies, concocted in a world which has been more thoroughly charted, and sometimes promoted by those who ought to know better – for example the *National Geographic*?

The Gentle Tasaday

In May 1971 a millionaire businessman in the Philippines called Manuel Elizalde, who had been made Presidential Assistant for Tribal Minorities by Ferdinand Marcos, announced that he had discovered a tribe in a remote part of Mindanao who were living in stone-age conditions. He called them the Tasaday and in July he took a hand-picked group of journalists and anthropologists to meet these survivors from a lost world. The party included a film crew sent out by *National Geographic,* who helped to get this particular ball rolling with an article entitled 'First Glimpse of a

---

[9]   *ibid.*, p.199.

[10] A. Smith, *The Wealth of Nations*, Book Four, Chapter Seven, first published 1776. Smith continues: 'More than a hundred years after the death of that great man, the Jesuit Gumila was still convinced of the reality of that wonderful country, and expressed with great warmth, and I dare to say, with great sincerity, how happy he should be to carry the gospel to a people who could so well reward the pious labours of their missionary.'

Stone Age Tribe', followed by a television documentary.[11] As news spread of the amazing discovery, academics, VIPs and journalists rushed to meet a genuine stone-age tribe – and sometimes to confirm their own deeply-held beliefs about the state of natural man, uncorrupted by society.[12] All visits were strictly controlled by Elizalde. He specified their timing and duration and told the favoured few what they could and could not ask. There was never any opportunity for serious and sustained scientific investigation.[13]

The success of Elizalde's method was shown in the line taken by an NBC documentary in 1972: 'They are non-aggressive, they have no religious rituals, they have neither art nor written language, they have no words for weapons, hostility or war'.[14] An American journalist called John Nance was head of Associated Press's Philippines bureau. He wrote up the story in a best-selling book called *The Gentle Tasaday*,[15] and found a new career lecturing, writing and broadcasting on the subject of these remarkable people, and how much they had to teach us.

---

[11] 'First Glimpse of a Stone Age Tribe', *National Geographic*, Vol. 140, No. 6, December 1971, pp.880-882. The TV documentary made by the *National Geographic* crew, *The Last Tribes of Mindanao*, containing 'the first films made of the newly discovered Tasaday tribe', was broadcast by CBS on 12 January 1972. *National Geographic* expanded its coverage with a photo-story showing the Tasaday in their 'caves' in its August 1972 issue called 'The Tasadays: Stone Age Cavemen of Mindanao' (K. MacLeish, Vol. 142 No. 2, pp.219-249.)

[12] This was certainly the spin which Elizalde put on it. 'Everyone goes around talking about people being bad because that's human nature. Well, I say that is crap. When you see these people, you have got to say, "No, man is not basically evil."' (Quoted in J. Nance, *The Gentle Tasaday: A Stone Age People in the Philippine Rain Forest*, New York: Harcourt Brace Jovanovich, 1975, p.75.)

[13] As Gerald Berreman makes clear in his chapter-and-verse account of the affair, the scientific investigation of the Tasaday involved, at most, 100 - 125 person-days, and this was made up of brief, spasmodic and closely supervised encounters by a dozen scientists, none of whom spoke or understood the language. (G.D. Berreman, 'The Incredible "Tasaday": Deconstructing the Myth of a "Stone-Age" People', *Cultural Survival Quarterly*, Vol. 15, 1991, pp.2-45.)

[14] 'The Cave People of the Philippines', NBC Reports, NBC-TV, 1972.

[15] J. Nance, *op.cit.*

In 1972 Ferdinand Marcos imposed martial law on the Philippines. A visit to the Tasaday by an Australian ethnobotanist in December 1972 was the last permitted by Elizalde, who later announced that the site was being closed in order to preserve the Tasaday from corruption by the outside world.[16] For 14 years the legend fermented until, in 1986, with Marcos overthrown and Elizalde forced to flee the country, a Swiss anthropologist called Oswald Iten, working in Manila, saw his chance. Realising that the conditions of civil unrest meant that the restricted access to the Tasaday site in Mindanao had probably been abandoned, he set off to do some further research. When he got there he found that the Tasaday were not wearing leaves, eating berries and living in caves: they were wearing Western clothes, practising agriculture, and living in huts. The whole thing had been a hoax. Inevitably, when he filed his story[17] he found himself challenged by all those who had invested their reputations in the Gentle Tasaday. Only a week after he had photographed the 'natives' in their jeans and T-shirts, a team from the German magazine *Stern,* arriving by prior arrangement, found them in native garb (mostly naked) again – except that one of the girls had not taken sufficient trouble to conceal her knickers with the 'native' skirt of leaves.[18] The *Stern* article still came to the conclusion that it was all a hoax, but this was followed by another contradictory article in *Asiaweek*, reporting a return visit by a group composed of Elizalde's chosen acolytes from the original 1971-2 expeditions, insisting that the whole story had been checked and verified.[19]

---

[16] In 1976 Marcos' Presidential Decree No. 1017 forbad entry to 'unexplored tribal grounds', specifically mentioning the 'Tasaday Reservation'.

[17] O. Iten, 'Die Tasaday - ein philippinsher Stinzeitschwindel, *Neue Zurcher Zeitung,* 12/13 April 1986, pp.77 - 79.

[18] W. Unger and J. Ullal, 'Der Grosse Bluff im Regenwald', *Stern,* Vol. 39, No. 17, pp.20-33, 179, April 1986.

[19] 'Controversies: Return to the Tasaday', *Asiaweek*, Vol. 12, No. 24, pp.26-38, 15 June 1986.

In 1988 Central TV made a documentary called *Scandal of the Lost Tribe*[20] for which they took a camera crew to the site and interviewed the Tasaday – except that they were not Tasaday at all. They were members of other tribes, mostly T'boli, and they spoke, with minor variations, the language commonly used in that part of Mindanao, not a 'unique' language. They certainly had words for 'war' and 'enemy'. They confirmed that they had been offered money, an improved standard of living, helicopters and other goodies on condition that they agreed to be 'stone-age' tribespeople. Whenever Western visitors were being brought to the site a messenger would be sent on ahead to tell them to get their clothes off and get into the caves.

In spite of mounting evidence of the hoax, the controversy has still not been resolved. Less than a year after the Central TV documentary, the BBC's Horizon programme[21] made another documentary which asked if the hoax story had been a hoax. Scientists defended their continuing belief in the authenticity of the Tasaday's primitive simplicity, but in one respect the Tasaday had proved themselves to be very modern in their outlook: they had learned how to use the media. There was by this time so much contradictory photographic evidence that it was obvious they were giving each visiting film crew the images they wanted: '...donning T-shirts and showing off their houses for ABC TV, reverting to the jungle and trees for NBC TV'.[22]

The most interesting aspect of the Gentle Tasaday story is not the question of who put them up to it and why.[23] It is the light which the whole incident throws on the behaviour of professors

---

[20] Broadcast 23 August 1988.

[21] Broadcast 20 March 1989.

[22] W. Holmes, 'Tribal truths', *The Times*, 21 March 1989.

[23] Aram Yengoyan has explained the fraud as part of the Marcos administration's plan to recreate Philippine culture, free from the 'contaminating' influences of Spain, the USA and Roman Catholicism: 'the Tasaday became pawns of a decadent oligarchy seeking a new lease for their reconstituted form of state and cultural hegemony'. ('Shaping and Reshaping the Tasaday: A question of Cultural Identity - a Review Article', *The Journal of Asian Studies*, Vol. 50, No. 3, August 1991, p.573.)

with passionate convictions. As Thomas Sutcliffe put it in *The Independent*:

> 'Imagine a tribe which believed that all human beings were essentially pristine and that all civilised behaviour, even something as rudimentary as cooking food, was a smear on an unsmirched, primal innocence. Far-fetched, perhaps, but such a tribe exists – they are called anthropologists.'[24]

The Land of Lost Content

Perhaps we should resist the temptation to laugh at people who go chasing after dreams. After all, it is a deeply ingrained human characteristic to want to leave behind the problems of this workaday world and set out in search of paradise.[25] Shakespeare painted a tempting picture of just such a bolthole, 'Under the Greenwood Tree':

> 'Who doth ambition shun,
> And loves to live i'th' sun,
> Seeking the food he eats,
> And pleas'd with what he gets,
> Come hither, come hither, come hither.
> Here shall he see
> No enemy
> But winter and rough weather.'[26]

We all want to believe that somewhere there is a magical kingdom waiting for us, down the rabbit-hole or over the rainbow, if only we could find the way in. Unfortunately, there is no Shangri-La nestling in the Himalayas, no Brigadoon about to materialise through the mists, and no Neverland, where old age can be kept at bay. These fantastic places exist only in our imaginations — harmless enough as retreats from reality, as

---

[24] T. Sutcliffe, 'Primal Scream', *The Independent*, 21 March 1989.

[25] As Richard North points out, the tourist industry is largely based on the mass-marketing of this fantasy. 'Travel brochures sell us paradise islands in which we can indulge many potent dreams...This is paradise as a theme park. Paradise has to some extent become a leisure pursuit, a holiday destination.' (R. North, *Life on a Modern Planet*, Manchester University Press, 1995, p.194.)

[26] *As You Like It*, Act II, Scene v.

holiday destinations where we can relax and revise our strategies for dealing with the demands of everyday life, but dangerous when they become confused with reality itself.

Regrettably, Utopia is not to be found, even in the best atlases. If it ever existed, it must have sunk beneath the waves long ago, like the lost continent of Atlantis. All that we are left with are ordinary men and women, neither noble nor ignoble, struggling in a generally hostile environment to do the best for themselves and their families. There are no doubt things which we can learn from native peoples about caring for the environment, and there are things which they can learn from us. It would be helpful if we could drop the stereotype of the noble savage, which must be amongst the oldest and most misleading in literature and anthropology, and just deal with the world and its peoples as they really are.

Index

Aborigines, 35, 53
Alvard, Michael, 51-2
Anderson, Terry, 38-9, 50

Bacon, Francis, 59
Bailey, David, 37n, 55
Behn, Aphra, 10-11, 18
Brazil, 2-5, 48-50, 59
Brunton, Ron, 45, 52-3
Burke, Edmund, 18
Butler, Samuel, 59

cannibalism, 4
Chase, Alston, 31, 34, 58
Cleland, John, 12-13, 18
Columbus, Christopher, 1-2, 7,
    28, 29, 30, 32, 41, 48, 61
    attitudes towards, 23-7
Cook, Captain, 9n, 37n, 47
Costner, Kevin, 42
Cowper, 47-8n

Demsetz, Harold, 38
Denevan, William, 29, 33, 39, 41-2
Dryden, John, ix, 10

Earth Summit, 1992, 32
Economist, The, 49
El Dorado, 60-2
Elizalde, Manuel, 62-4

Feest, Christian, 45-6
Ferdinand, King, 1, 2, 48

Garden of Eden, 1, 5, 9n, 23, 27, 28
Glover, Mark, 57
Green movement, 20-3
Greenpeace, 57

Hawaii, 36-7

International Planned Parenthood
    Federation, 37
International Union for the
    Conservation of Nature, 51
Inuit, 56-7
Isabella, Queen, 1, 2, 48

James I, 61
Johnson, Paul, 17
Johnson, Samuel, 47n

Kaufman, Wallace, 23, 36-7
Kay, Charles, 40-1
Kayapo Indians, 48-50, 54-5

Lawrence, D.H., 19
Leo XIII, Pope, 24
Locke, John, 20
Lovelock, James, 21n
Lynx, 37, 57-8

Madagascar, 35
Malaysia, 52
Maoris, 36
Marcos, Ferdinand, 62-4
Martin, Peter, 36

Mead, Margaret, 13-15
Micmac Indians, 48, 58
Montaigne, Michel de, 2-6, 8, 9, 16-7, 26
Montesquieu, vii
More, Sir Thomas, 59-60
Morris, William, 59

National Geographic, 26, 62
Nichol, Charles, 61
Nietzsche, 19
North, Richard D., 23

Omai, 47-8
Orinoco River, 1, 61
overkill hypothesis, 36
Ovid, 4, 5

Perry, Ted, 43-4
Piro, 51-2
Plato, 5n, 59
Pocahontas, 42

Raleigh, Sir Walter, 60-2
Rangel, Carlos, 6, 18-9
Ridley, Matt, 15, 36
Roddick, Anita, 47
Ronsard, 2
Rousseau, Jean-Jacques, 15-9, 26, 47
Royal, Robert, 23, 26, 27, 40

Sale, Kirkpatrick, 26-7, 28
Sallust, 1
Seattle, Chief, 42-5
Semang, 52
Shakespeare, William
    The Tempest, 7-9
    As You Like It, 66

Smith, Adam, 62
Smithsonian Institution, 28
Stearman, Allyn McLean, 53, 55n
Sting, 48-50
Swift, Jonathan, 59

Tahiti, 9n
Tasaday tribe, 62-6

Venezuela, 1, 27, 60, 62
Virgil, 4, 5
Voltaire, vii, 16n

Washington, George, 44
Wells, H.G., 59
Wilde, Oscar, 25n, 28, 58, 59, 60

Yuqui Indians, 53-4